The Busy Person's Guide to Preserving Food

Janet Bachand Chadwick

The Busy Person's Guide to Preserving Food

Janet Bachand Chadwick

A Storey Publishing Book

Storey Communications, Inc.
Schoolhouse Road
Pownal, Vermont 05261

The mission of Storey Communications is to serve our customers
by publishing practical information that encourages personal
independence in harmony with the environment.

Revised and updated by Andrea Chesman
Edited by Gwen W. Steege
Cover and text design by Cindy McFarland
Cover photograph by Nicholas Whitman
Text production by Wanda Harper Joyce and Susan Bernier
Line drawings by Elayne Sears
Indexed by Northwind Editorial Services

Printed in the United States by R.R. Donnelley
First Printing, June 1995

Library of Congress Cataloging-in-Publication Data

Chadwick, Janet, 1933-
    The busy person's guide to preserving food / Janet Bachand
Chadwick. -- [Rev. and updated]
            p.   cm.
    "A Storey Publishing book."
    Includes bibliographical references and index.
    ISBN 0-88266-900-1 (pb)
    1. Food--Preservation. I. Title.
TX601.C43   1995
641.4—dc20   95-11845
                                                            CIP

Contents

~

~

Acknowledgments

~

I would like to thank Louellan Wasson, home economist, for her technical editing and moral support throughout the writing of this book. Many others deserve thanks, too: Andrea Chesman, my editor, who had the original idea for this book; Mary Clark of Garden Way, for obtaining many new items of food processing equipment for me to test; Moulinex and General Electric companies, in particular Mr. Ted Miller of General Electric Co., for making available to me food processors for testing; Lynn Liberty of Garden Way Living Center, for her never-failing support; Win Way, University of Vermont Extension Agronomist, for his educated palate; and Elayne Sears for her descriptive illustrations.

Last but not least, I'd like to thank my family, especially my husband, Raymond, for taking on extra gardening chores to help make this book possible, and to my daughter, Kim, for her all-around help.

The Busy Person's Dilemma

YOU HAVE THREE CHILDREN UNDER FIVE, the baby cried all night, and your mother-in-law is coming for supper. What are you going to do with that bushel of green beans? . . . Or, it's Thursday, and you just arrived home after a hard day at the office. You know that if you wait until Saturday to make dill pickles, the cucumbers will be too large; but if you pick them now, they will be punky by Saturday . . . but you don't feel like pickling until midnight. What are you going to do? Well, take a deep breath and relax. *This* book is for you.

Vegetable gardening is rapidly becoming the number one American pastime. Escalating food costs, inferior quality products, and chemical additives have convinced many of us that the best way to provide good food at reasonable costs for our families is to raise it ourselves.

When calculating the savings of a garden and home food processing, many people (always non-gardeners) will remark, "Yes, but how much is your time worth?" To answer that question you have to be honest with yourself. Would you really be holding down an extra job during those hours that would *net* you more cash in the bank? Can you put a price tag on the physical, emotional, and spiritual satisfactions that you derive from working the soil and producing the foods that nourish your family? Is the kind of food you feed your family important to you? Is there any way you can "buy" the feeling of pride you have when you show off the full freezer; the rows of canned vegetables, fruits, pickles, jams, and jellies; or the root cellar shelves filled to the ceiling? If these things are not important to you, then maybe you should not be gardening or preserving food; because there *is* a lot of work involved — but the work should be a joy and a challenge to your ability to be more self-reliant.

I've written this book for those of you who garden and hold down outside jobs, or are busy with youngsters and other outside activities. I know that it is hard enough to cope with the normal routine of family, home, and job, along with raising a small garden for fresh summer vegetables, without trying to squeeze in long hours of food preservation at the end of a busy day. But much food can be preserved for storage in the small blocks of time you have available on a daily or weekly basis. This book can be used as a primer if you are new to the art of food preservation, and it may bring new and exciting ideas to those of you who have been preserving food for years.

How Can This Book Help You?

Freezing is the most popular method of food preservation. It's the most time-saving method, and it produces the best finished product; and so this book will focus strongly on freezing techniques, including some new methods that are even more time-saving and produce an even better finished product.

Drying is an ancient method of preserving food, and it is a method that is gaining in popularity as people discover how much they enjoy having an inexpensive supply of "gourmet" Italian dried tomatoes and kid-pleasing fruit leathers. Also, as more and more people grow their own herbs, they find drying a convenient way of preserving that harvest. So I will give plenty of advice for drying fruits, vegetables, and herbs.

I will discuss the equipment that is absolutely necessary for food preservation, and I will add information on other equipment that, while not absolutely necessary, will make food preservation faster, easier, and, in general, give a better finished product.

People who are serious about food preservation should realize that many steps can be taken year-round to make harvest time easier. Throughout the book I will give you tips that will help you to make the best use of weekends, weekdays, and overnight hours. These tips will include the best times to harvest vegetables as well as the best ways to keep them fresh for up to three days, so that you can plan to harvest one day and preserve a day or so later.

Since I can already hear nutritionists raising their voices in a collective uproar over this last remark, I think I'd better explain myself. Many commercially sold fresh vegetables and fruits are treated with chemicals to preserve their *look* of freshness; they can be from two days to two weeks old when they appear in your market. You have no way of knowing how many times frozen foods have been defrosted and refrozen (losing nutrients and flavor) before they appear in the frozen food cases of your market. Nor is there any way to judge the hours or days that lapsed between the harvest and processing of canned foods. You will never know what chemicals were sprayed on these foods while they were growing.

Obviously, you can't possibly get anything worse than what you buy in a supermarket, so you are already ahead of the game. Even though the *best* way to preserve all the nutrients and fresh flavor of foods is to pick them at their peak and process them immediately, you can be sure that waiting even two days between harvest and processing will not cost you much more than minimal loss of either nutrients or flavor *if you follow my instructions on storing*. Therefore, you have nothing to lose and everything to gain by preserving your food by my methods.

I will give step-by-step, illustrated instructions for processing each commonly grown vegetable and fruit. I will give recipes for catsup, salsa, pickles, jams, jellies, and herbal vinegars.

I will include food preparation ideas and recipes for delicious meals that can be prepared ahead of harvest time to make busy days much easier. I will also share my recipes that incorporate the vegetables being preserved for quick and easy harvest meals.

In addition to all this, I will include a list of reference books on gardening and food preservation that can be read during the winter leisure hours any time.

There are three important pieces of advice I'd like to share before we get into serious food preservation. First, take the time to excite the entire family with the real meaning of what you are accomplishing for yourselves, and how their independence will make them stand taller in a world that is so filled with deprivation. It will make the harder days easier for everyone to cope with. A good attitude is insurance against discouragement when you are tired. Second, stay flexible. This is important mostly from a psychological standpoint. If you become too rigid in your expectations, you will waste tremendous amounts of emotional energy trying to keep up, or being disappointed at failures. This can ruin the best of goals. Finally, know yourself. If you work best at night, plan your work for the evening hours; but if you are a morning person, get up an hour or so earlier in the morning to accomplish extra tasks.

The following pages are packed with information to help you make the best use of your time and resources during the harvest season. Good luck and have fun!

CHAPTER

1

Taking the Mystery
Out of Equipment

PEA SHELLERS, APPLE PEELERS, cherry pitters, food mills, food processors, microwave ovens: Are they really time-savers in the harvest kitchen?

If you are serious about making food preservation as quick and easy as possible, you will want to invest in some time-saving equipment. The right equipment not only makes work easier and more enjoyable, but the end results are usually better, so the feeling of satisfaction is greater.

You do not need to purchase the most expensive equipment on the market; there are some very good and reliable products sold at reasonable prices. A good food processor is just about the best helping hand a busy person can have at harvest time. Prices range from as low as $45, all the way up to $200 for one of the best Cuisinart models with all the attachments. Once you realize what a help this type of appliance will be to you throughout the year, you will probably see it as a good investment. On the other hand, every new gadget that you see advertised may not be worth the money. In this chapter I will concentrate on the food-processing items that I have tested and found useful in my kitchen.

Determine Your Needs First

Before you step into a store or look through a catalog, you should have a good idea of just what equipment you need. What you need is

Basic Equipment List

For Root Cellaring: The Fastest Method

boxes   large plastic bags
barrels   crocks

For Freezing:
A High-Quality, Convenient End Product

freezer

scrub brush

strainers — fine sieves and colanders

paring and chopping knives

food processing equipment — grinders, slicers, blenders, or food processors

measuring cups and spoons

wide-mouth funnel

timer

hot pads, mitts, or heavy potholders

heavy bath towels

large bowls

large roaster or kettle

cookie sheets or jelly roll pans for tray-freezing

freezer containers and bags

For Drying: It Takes Time, but Little Effort

Everything on the freezing list, plus
a dehydrator or oven

For Canning in a Boiling Water Bath:
Pickles, Preserves, Tomatoes, and Fruit

Everything on Freezing list plus

boiling water bath canner

preserving kettle

tea kettle

soup ladle

nonmetallic spatula or wooden chopstick

large wooden and slotted spoons

jar lifter or tongs

canning jars and lids

determined by the foods you will prepare and the methods of preservation you will use. Will you freeze? Can? Pickle? Store in a root cellar? Dry? Will you need to chop? Slice? Dice? Grind? Or puree?

If you haven't decided just how you will be preserving your harvest, glance ahead to chapters 3, 4, and 5 to decide which methods you will be trying. There is no point in investing in equipment you won't use.

The Expensive Appliances

In my kitchen, I have found that I really save time by using my freezer, dishwasher, food processor, and microwave oven. Of course, you can preserve food without these appliances, but their year-round uses justify their costs.

Freezers: A Major Investment

Although a freezer is a major investment, freezing is very often the fastest method of food processing, and it generally gives you a product that is closest to fresh.

Small freezers contained in refrigerators are not cold enough to freeze and store foods. Your freezer must be a separate unit that maintains a temperature of at least 0°F or lower to inhibit the growth of bacteria, yeasts, and molds, and to stop the enzyme action that can cause discoloration and destroy the fresh flavor of frozen foods.

Costs. It is not necessary to consider only nationally advertised brand-name models when you buy a new freezer. There are operating costs associated with freezers which you should take into consideration. New energy-efficient models cost much less per year to operate than older models, a consideration if you are contemplating a used freezer. Each new freezer should list the approximate amount of energy the unit consumes per year, so be sure to do some comparison shopping. Self-defrosting freezers may not cost more to operate than manual-defrosting models. Accumulated frost in a manual-defrosting model acts as an insulator between the cooling coils and the interior, so that additional energy is required to keep the unit cold and to recool the entire freezer after it has been defrosted.

Chest Freezers Versus Upright Freezers. Chest freezers tend to be colder since cold air does not rise quickly when the lid is raised. They hold more food overall per cubic foot and usually cost less than upright models. Upright freezers use less floor space, and they make reaching for food more convenient. But cold air spills from them when the doors are opened; therefore, operating costs are greater. Much of the space in an upright goes to waste since it must be packed so that food won't fall out when the door is opened.

Microwave Ovens Perform Many Tasks

Microwaves perform many time-saving functions when it comes to preserving food. Where they really shine is in the preparation work for freezing — blanching vegetables and heating sugar syrups. They are also quite handy for cooking fruits before pureeing for fruit leathers. And, of course, microwaves are great for the year-round tasks of cooking fresh and frozen vegetables for the table and rehydrating dried foods.

There are limits to the versatility of the microwave, however, and it should not be used for making preserves or drying most foods, despite the recommendations of some people. There are books that have recipes for microwave preserves; these recipes usually work in quantities no greater than 4 cups of fruit. The cooking times are comparable to larger batches done on top of the stove, and there is a tendency for the boiling hot fruit mixture to boil over the top of the cooking container and make a mess inside the oven. Also, a tremendous amount of steam is generated, which can be hazardous.

Microwave drying is not recommended by some oven manufacturers, as removing all of the moisture from the oven creates what's known as a "no-load" situation that can damage the machine's magnetron tube over time. Microwave drying can also cause a "volcanic effect." That is, the food feels very hot and dry on the outside, but is still moist on the inside. If stored, this moisture can turn into mold or cause the food to become rancid. In addition, the intensity of a microwave makes it very easy to overdry foods, resulting in a burned or charred flavor. Some foods, such as herbs, may even catch on fire.

So while it is possible to dry foods in a microwave oven, it is not always wise. Be sure to consult your machine's instructions before attempting to use it to dry foods or herbs.

The microwave should never be used to sterilize jars for canning — it just doesn't do the job.

Dehydrators Produce the Highest-Quality Dried Foods

Do you really need this extra piece of equipment? Well, no. But after a few seasons of drying food in your oven or air-drying above your woodstove or outside in the sun — if you live in a hot, dry, sunny climate — you may find that the ease of drying and the convenience of dried foods make drying your favorite method of preservation. Then it will be time to invest in this handy appliance. Dehydrators range in price from about $30 to $100.

Like other kitchen appliances, home food dehydrators come in an array of sizes, shapes, and colors, with a wide assortment of features. The basic components of an effective dehydrator include a heat source, a fan to circulate the heat and remove moist air, and trays for the food. Also helpful is a thermostat to regulate the temperature from a low of about 100°F (for herbs) to a high of about 140°F (for meats). A timer that will turn off the dehydrator is a highly desirable feature.

When choosing a size, consider how much counter space you can allow for it when in use, and how much storage space you have when it is not in use. Also, consider how much drying space you will want. As a rule of thumb, 12 square feet of drying area is sufficient for a half-bushel of vegetables.

Food Processors Save Time

Food processors work so fast that washing the vegetables, cutting them to size, and placing them in the feed tube takes more time than the actual processing. This versatile appliance combines many of the functions of the blender, grinder, and slicer. While processors do not puree as efficiently as blenders, they do a creditable job. They

Side-chute food processor

will also grind coffee and meat, and slice, julienne, shred, and grate. Many have accessories that will allow you to cut and ripple cut french fries. They make breads, pie crusts, and sauces with just a flick of the wrist. They can be taken apart easily for cleaning, and most parts are dishwasher safe.

Which Food Processor to Buy. There are two basic types of processors: direct-drive, which means that the bowl and blades sit directly on top of the motor's shaft; and belt-driven, where the bowl mounts to one side of the motor. The belt-driven types take up more counter space than the direct-drive processors, and the belt-driven machines that I have tested seem to overheat faster than those with direct-drive.

Most food processors feed the chopped, diced, or sliced vegetables into a bowl. The larger the bowl, the fewer times you will have to empty the vegetables into a larger bowl, and the less time your work will take.

Blenders, Strainers, Food Mills, and Other Useful (and Useless) Tools

Before the electric food processor, there were many electric and manual appliances that made food processing easy. I still use my hand-cranked Squeezo strainer and wouldn't be without it. Here are a few appliances you may want to use during the harvest season.

Blender

Blenders

Blenders have become almost a standard appliance in most kitchens. They can be used to mince, chop, grate, puree, or just blend. They are not as efficient as food processors for coarsely chopping or grating vegetables, since they tend to chop too finely; however, they do a better job of pureeing than the food processor. Blenders often are easier to clean than food processors.

Strainers and Food Mills

If you make your own tomato juice, sauce, or puree; make soup purees; freeze winter squash or pumpkins; or make your own applesauce, you will not want to be without a good strainer or food mill during the harvest season.

There are three basic types of strainers and mills, but if you preserve large quantities of food, the best is the type that uses hand-cranked augers to crush the food and force it through perforated, cone-shaped strainers or screens. Large hoppers direct the purees into bowls, while augers move the skins, seeds, and cores into waste

Squeezo strainer

bowls at the other end. To process apples in these strainers, just quarter and cook them until tender. Tomatoes can be quartered and pureed uncooked. I can strain 7 quarts of tomato puree in just 10 minutes in my hand-cranked strainer, and the finished product is excellent.

These strainers are meant for large jobs, and they take a little extra time for clean-up. All parts can be washed in the dishwasher. The strainer screens, which are the hardest part to clean, can be cleaned quickly and easily by forcing a large canning jar scrub brush down inside the straining screen and giving it a few twists. Before removing the brush, scrub the outside of the screen with a small stiff-bristled brush.

The smaller Foley Food Mill, shaped like a 2-quart saucepan with holes in the bottom, has a handle with a horizontal cranking arm that operates a semi-circular disk that forces the food through the holes. Underneath, a spring-loaded wire scrapes the bottom clean. Releasing a nut on the bottom allows it to come apart easily for cleaning. The Foley Food Mill doesn't work efficiently on items with tough skins. For instance, tomato skins and seeds tend to get clogged in the bottom. By reversing the action of the disk, however, it can be unclogged quite easily, and you can either remove the skins or continue straining. Foley Food Mills are readily available wherever kitchenware is sold.

Food mill

Bean frencher

There are chinois strainers — cone-shaped strainers with pestles — that come in aluminum or stainless steel. A large wooden pestle, made to fit snugly in the bottom of the cone, presses food against the sides to squeeze it through. Tomato seeds are frequently forced through the holes, giving the tomato puree a speckled look. These strainers cost under $20.

For making clear fruit juices, you will need a jelly bag or cheesecloth for straining out fruit pulp. These can be set inside a colander or strainer. (Cheesecloth is also needed to cover food that is being dried outside.)

Slicers

There are a variety of manually operated vegetable and cabbage slicers on the market costing anywhere from a few dollars to under $50. While they can't possibly be as efficient as a food processor, they still produce a nice product with less effort than slicing with a knife.

Bean Slicers

My food processor does such a good job of julienne-slicing beans with the thin-slice blade that I would never use anything else. I can do a bushel of beans julienne-style in 35 minutes. However, not all food processors do as good a job. If I had to buy a bean slicer, I would purchase the little hand-held Krisk that sells for only $5. It is slow, but it does the best job.

Apple peeler

Apple Peelers

There are several apple peelers on the market; some work better than others. Ask for a demonstration before you purchase one. I consider my apple peeler a nice extra, not a necessary piece of equipment. Unless you put up bushels of sliced apples, you will not find much use for a peeler.

Thermometers

If you are planning to make jams and jellies, or to can fruit juices, a thermometer is very, very useful. Although there are plenty of tests for determining when jelly has gelled, nothing is as reliable as a good thermometer.

Bag sealer

Freezing Aids

Boilable plastic bags and automatic sealers are not new to the market, but they haven't achieved the popularity they deserve. In fact, you may only find them through mail-order companies that specialize in products for gardeners (see Appendix). In my opinion, boilable bags are one of the best ideas in a long time. They can be used for freezing fresh produce, leftovers, or freshly made casseroles, soups, and stews in single-size portions to be reheated later, right in the boilable bag. They have been reviewed by the FDA and found to be completely safe for processing and cooking foods.

If your only experience with boilable bags has been with commercially frozen foods that you reheated in the bag, and you have not been pleased with the results, give home-processed bags a second chance. As you will see in chapter 4, you can save a lot of time when freezing vegetables by packing the prepared vegetables in the bag, then blanching, cooling, and freezing — right in the bag. When it comes time to cook the vegetables, you can reheat them in the bag, but some are best steamed or stir-fried.

The boilable bags are made of heavy-duty, food-safe plastic, and most sealers work by placing the top of the bag on a small, heated sealing strip inside the appliance. Some sealers are designed to use continuous rolls so that you can custom-cut the size bag you need. There are other models that will seal different foods in separate sections of the same bag, allowing you to put together an entire meal at a time.

Some manufacturers offer a vacuum seal feature on their sealing units. These sealers are more expensive. Although they do a good job of sealing, it is a waste of money to purchase a vacuum sealer for freezing vegetables since even the best machines cannot remove all the air.

You do not have to invest in a bag sealer. You can fill a boilable bag, place the bag on a heavy bath towel over the edge of a counter, cover the bag with a damp cloth, and seal with an electric iron set on low. The electric iron isn't as convenient as the automatic bag sealer, but trying the process with an iron will let you know whether you want to invest in the equipment.

Blanchers, Preserving Kettles, and Canners

5-in-1 steam blancher

The pots in which you blanch vegetables, cook down relishes and jams, and process canned foods are necessary pieces of equipment. But before you buy anything new, be sure that you will need these pots.

Blanchers

The traditional way of preparing vegetables for the freezer is to blanch the vegetables in boiling water to cover, cool them, drain, then bag. It is not the fastest way — using the boilable bag method is, as we will see in chapter 3.

There is one blancher on the market that is so handy I find many uses for it, even though I blanch most of my vegetables in the microwave. The 5-in-1 Pot Steam Blancher is a versatile little kettle made up of a 7-quart deep pan, a deep steam basket, a smaller colander-type of basket, a flat, perforated container that holds about 2 cups, and a cover. It can be used for cooking and steam blanching (three layers at a time), and the colander can be used for straining. It's the handiest pot in my kitchen and sells for about $30.

For blanching vegetables in a microwave, one pound at a time, you will need a 2-quart, microwave-safe container.

If your microwave container does not have a lid, you will have to cover the container with microwave-safe plastic wrap. The microwave-safe plastic wraps that contain polyvinyl chloride form the best seals. Use a big enough piece to allow for steam to collect inside the wrap. To safely remove the wrap from hot food, pierce the plastic with the tip of a knife to release the steam and peel the plastic up and away from the container.

Preserving Kettles

A heavy-bottomed, large-capacity pot is needed for making jams, jellies, and pickles, and for cooking down purees to make fruit leathers. It should be made of a nonreactive metal — that is, stainless steel, enamel-clad cast-iron, anodized aluminum, or most nonstick finishes. These materials will not be affected by the acid in citrus juice, vinegar, fruit, or tomatoes. Pots made of unlined aluminum, copper, or cast iron may react with acidic foods to produce an off flavor or to discolor the food. The heavy bottom is necessary to disperse the heat evenly and prevent scorching, which is particularly important when you are making jams and chutneys.

Boiling Water Bath Canners

Also called "cold-pack canners," boiling water bath canners can be used to process acid foods only. They come in two sizes — the smaller one can process up to 7 quarts at a time, and the larger size can process 9 quarts. They can be made of stainless steel, aluminum, or porcelain-on-steel — the latter being the least expensive, selling for $15 to $25. Any large kettle can be used in place of this type of canner as long as it is as deep as a quart canning jar, plus 4 inches. It should have a cover in order to keep up a good rolling boil throughout the canning process.

Miscellanous Items You Probably Already Own

A set of glass measuring cups is useful for measuring and pouring hot jellies, thin sauces, sugar syrups, and brines. They have the advantage of being safe for the microwave. Likewise, it's handy to have more than one set of measuring spoons, particularly when you are measuring a lot of different ingredients for pickles and relishes.

Final Thoughts

If you were to ask me what equipment I considered indispensable in my harvest kitchen, I would answer without hesitation: my freezer, dishwasher, food processor, hand-cranked strainer, and blender. I purchased each of these appliances as soon as they became available for home use, and I can assure you that over the years, they have paid for themselves many times over.

A dishwasher is one of the best time-saving appliances that you can invest in. It will wash several batches of canning or freezing jars at once and keep them hot until needed. Also, dishwashers are a help with the everyday clean-up chores that need to be done during all seasons.

A dehydrator for less than $100 is a good alternative to a freezer, but a freezer allows you to save time and produce a more palatable end product.

There are many more gadgets and appliances on the market. Most are worthless, but occasionally, something good comes along. If you find an item that looks like it might work for you, and you can afford it, give it a try. After all, it's the fun of experimenting that takes our daily lives out of the ordinary.

TIP *If you cannot afford some of the larger pieces of food processing equipment, you might consider getting together with two or three friends and share the cost. This will mean that you must either stagger harvest dates or plan to process foods together in sort of a mini-cooperative.*

TIP *As you buy new kitchen appliances, put the directions for assembly and use, parts order slips, and warranties in a drawer; or make up a loose-leaf binder with them, and put it with your cookbooks. This will save time when using these appliances for the first few times, to say nothing of the aggravation that comes from looking for these papers when they are scattered all over, or when you need to have the appliance repaired.*

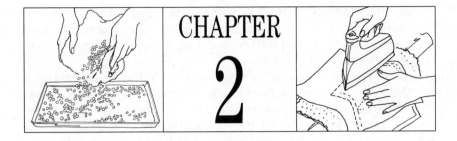

CHAPTER 2

Tips, Hints, and Other Shortcuts

The *best* way to preserve fruits and vegetables is to pick them at the peak of their maturity and bring them from garden to freezer or dehydrator or canner immediately. However, for many of us this is *almost* impossible. I emphasize "almost" because, with proper advance planning, you can find the time for food preservation. "But," you ask, "all the planning in the world won't prevent the green beans from ripening in the middle of the week when I have the least amount of time. Then what do I do?"

10 Harvesting Tips

Timing planting. If you stagger the planting dates of vegetables, they won't all be ready at the same time. This will make it easy to harvest and process small batches of vegetables frequently in short blocks of time.

Timing picking. Vegetables picked late in the afternoon or early in the evening (with a few exceptions) will keep better. They have been manufacturing natural sugars and nutrients all day; once the sun goes down, they will use up part of these sugars and nutrients and are at their low ebb early in the morning.

Quality. Pick only the best vegetables for storing. Use bruised or less perfect produce for daily meals.

Avoid bruising. When picking produce, handle with care to prevent bruising.

Morning picking. Berries keep better if they are picked early in the day.

Shallow containers. When picking berries, collect the fruit in small containers to avoid packed and crushed fruit. As soon as each small container is filled, place it in the shade.

Short-term storage. Store small amounts of fruits and vegetables in a refrigerator or ice chest. Place berries in colanders when refrigerating.

Short-term storage in large cans. Large plastic or metal garbage cans, with holes punched in the bottom for drainage, make good containers for extra produce when they are filled with ice. Put a layer of ice in the bottom, and cover with folded newspapers. Place the fresh fruit or vegetables in plastic bags on the newspapers, then place another layer of ice on the bags, and cover with more newspapers to keep in the cold. Set the can in a shady, protected spot. This will keep produce fresh for 2 to 3 days. Add fresh ice daily.

Short-term storage in appliances. Fruits and vegetables, along with large ice packs or plastic jugs of ice wrapped in plastic bags to prevent leaking (condensation forms on the outside of jugs of ice), can be stored temporarily in your dishwasher, electric clothes dryer, or electric oven. (Do not use gas ovens with pilot lights.) Place a heavy towel in the bottom of the appliance; add the ice, then the fruits or vegetables. The insulation that prevents heat loss from these appliances will also keep in the cold. If you must store the produce for longer than 24 hours, change the ice. Return the melted ice packs or jugs to the freezer and refreeze for another time.

Washing. Do not wash fruits and vegetables that will be stored before processing. Wash when you are ready to freeze, dry, or can.

18 Preserving Tips

You will find most of my tips for saving time in chapters 3, 4, and 5 where I talk about specific ways of preserving food. Here are just a few reminders.

Plastic bags. Store harvested vegetables in plastic bags and cool immediately. Use several smaller bags rather than a single large one to help prevent bruising.

Tray-freezing vegetables. If you find yourself faced with mounds of vegetables and not enough time to process the lot of them, try tray-freezing them. Wash the vegetables, and dice or chop. (The smaller the pieces are, the faster they will freeze.) Spread the vegetables out on a few cookie sheets, place in the coolest part of your freezer, and allow to freeze. Once frozen, pour the vegetables into plastic bags. Chopped fresh vegetables can be frozen without blanching to be used within two months, if they are to be used in relishes or sauces. There is a little loss in the crisp texture of the relish, but few people will notice it. Make sure when defrosting that all the juices are collected in a bowl and used in the recipe as part of the liquid.

Tray-freezing berries. The fastest way to preserve berries is to wash them in cold water, *lift* the berries from the water, place in a colander, and drain well. Tray-freeze without sugar. When frozen solid, pack loosely in freezer bags. These berries can be used as you would use fresh berries for jams, jellies, pies, puddings, and sauces.

Applesauce. The fastest and easiest method of making applesauce is with a hand-cranked strainer. Apples need not be peeled or cored, just cooked until soft and pureed in the strainer. Applesauce can be frozen or canned.

Quality fruit. Use only firm, unblemished fruit to freeze for pies, fruit compotes, and shortcakes. Soft, overripe fruit will turn to mush when defrosted.

Purees. Overripe, unblemished fruits can be frozen sliced or whole (if small) to make quick purees when defrosted. Pop the defrosted fruits into a blender or food processor to make a smooth puree in an instant. Strain only if a very smooth puree is desired.

Juice into jelly. Another way to deal with mounds of fruits that have ripened all at once is to freeze or can them as juices to be made into jellies when you have the time.

Pumpkins and squash. Even if you don't have a proper root cellar, you can store pumpkins and winter squash until late in the fall or winter when you have more time for processing. Keep the squash and pumpkins on a closet floor after curing, and they will keep well for 2 to 3 months in these dark, cooler places.

Tree fruits. Apples, peaches, and pears should be sliced into a bowl of water containing lemon juice or ascorbic acid to prevent darkening. When all the fruit is prepared, drain well, and tray freeze or can in syrup.

Preparing syrups for fruits. Prepare syrup for syrup-packed frozen fruits and berries ahead of time when you have a few extra minutes; it will save time when preserving the fruits.

Heating syrups for fruits. I like to use an electric coffee maker to reheat and keep syrup hot for preserving fruit. The handle and pouring spout make it easy to fill jars. Older metal percolators should be cleaned by adding 2 tablespoons of vinegar to a pot of water and running it through a full cycle. *Caution:* Owners of automatic drip coffee makers should place syrup directly *into* coffee pots. *Do not put syrup in water well to reheat.*

Microwaving syrups. Sugar syrups can also be made in glass measuring cups and heated in the microwave. Just heat until the mixture boils, stirring once halfway through the cooking time. Remove and stir to make sure the sugar has completely dissolved. You can hold the syrup for up to 60 minutes with the oven set on WARM (10% power).

Clearest jellies. To obtain a very clear jelly, strain fruit in muslin bags overnight. Do not press the fruit in the bag. If juice remains in the fruit, press the fruit in another bowl to extract the extra juice. Use this second extraction for another batch of less clear jelly.

Avoid crystallization. To eliminate the problem of sugar crystals in freezer jams and jellies, measure the prepared fruit into a food processor, add sugar, and blend for 30 seconds. Let the fruit stand in the food processor for the length of time specified in the recipe, add the pectin mixture, and blend again for 30 seconds.

Firm strawberries. To keep strawberries from absorbing large quantities of water, do not hull them before washing.

Seedless jams. To remove seeds from berries and grapes for jams and conserves, puree in the Squeezo strainer with the berry strainer.

Defrosting berries. The best way to defrost tray-frozen berries is to place them in a bowl and cover with whatever sweetener you will be using in your recipe; do not stir. Cover the bowl tightly. This prevents exposure to air, and the berries retain better color, texture, and flavor.

Fruit pies and muffins. To make pies or muffins using tray-frozen fruits or berries, do not defrost before adding to the pie crust or batter. Add a few extra minutes to the baking time for muffins and 15 to 20 minutes for pies. This may necessitate covering the edges of the pie crust with foil for the first part of the baking time to prevent overbaked edges. Increase the amount of thickening for berry pies by half again as much. For example, if your recipe calls for 2 tablespoons of quick-cooking tapioca, add 3 tablespoons.

9 Tips for Setting Up an Efficient Work Flow

Arrange your kitchen for greater efficiency prior to the harvest season. Having a place for everything and knowing where everything is will save time, work, and frustration. Here are some suggestions:

Stow seasonal items. Pack away seasonal dishes and entertainment items that take up a lot of shelf or cupboard space to free kitchen space for better harvest time use. Plastic laundry baskets make good storage containers for out-of-season items because they can be labeled and stacked in a small area.

Eat elsewhere. If possible, set up a dining area for your family in a room other than your kitchen to allow you to keep your work area set up at all times during the heaviest part of the harvest season.

Use a picnic table. If possible, bring a picnic table into your kitchen for a large work area. The tops of most of these tables are just the right thickness for clamping on food processing equipment. I have found that if you are a short person, it is less tiring to use equipment with a crank handle on these tables because they are slightly lower than the average counter.

Shoe-bag holder. Hook a shoe bag with deep pockets to the inside of a door off your kitchen or pantry to hold small kitchen tools.

Sink-side cutting board. Make yourself a cutting board to fit over your sink. Use 1-inch pine cut slightly larger than the well of your sink. In one corner, cut out a 4-inch square hole with a jigsaw. (Outlining the area to be cut with masking tape will prevent the wood from splintering while it is being cut.) Place a plastic dishpan or bowl under the hole. As you peel and chop, the waste goes directly into the waste container to save time and messy clean-ups.

Herb-and-spice assortment. Make sure you have plenty of fresh herbs and spices. Take the time to mark the date on new containers as you open them. Once opened, herbs and ground spices should be used within 6 months, and whole spices within 1 year. After that they should be discarded because they lose flavor.

Spice storage. Use the inside doors on kitchen cupboards to mount spice racks. They won't collect dust and grease and will keep spices and herbs visible and quickly accessible. Line up spices and herbs in alphabetical order.

Closet storage spaces. Closets are usually dark and cooler than the rest of the house, so they make good food storage spaces. Make use of the backs of closet doors for food storage. Inexpensive racks are available that will hold as many as 50 to 55 quart jars. Steel canning shelves that will fit in large closets will hold up to 220 quart jars.

Lazy Susan. To fill jam and jelly jars quickly and easily, set the jars to be filled on a lazy Susan next to your preserve kettle. Rotate the lazy Susan as you fill the jars.

21 Ways to Make Life Easier During the Harvest

If gardening and food preservation are to be an important part of your life, take steps to fit them smoothly into your schedule. Many things can be done year-round to make the harvest season less frantic and tiring. These shortcuts can be incorporated into your regular work schedule, and you won't even miss the few extra minutes that most of these tasks take.

Planning calendar. Start by obtaining a calendar with large empty squares. Plan your year-round activities dealing with food preservation, and mark the times for these activities on this calendar. Variations or cancellations will occur, but important projects won't be forgotten and will be done on time.

Fall through Late Winter

Buying equipment. Shop for food preservation equipment in the fall to save time and money. Food preservation equipment usually goes on sale right after the harvest season.

Involve the whole family. Take the time to teach each member of the family how to do simple jobs: set the table, clear away after meals, run the dishwasher, do the laundry, make beds, dust, vacuum, and so on. Teach others in the family to do the grocery shopping by taking them with you a few times to learn the layout of the store, understand unit pricing, and be ready to share shopping chores at the busiest harvest time.

Stock up on stock. Make soup stocks to store in the freezer for quick, fresh vegetable soups in the summer. This is especially good if you heat with wood or coal stoves; you can use the energy for cooking that you are already using to heat your home.

Plan crops for use. Plan the types of foods you want to preserve before you plan your garden. For instance, if you plan to can or freeze large quantities of tomato juice, any good tomato will do. On the other hand, if catsup, spaghetti sauce, or chili sauce are desired, Italian plum tomatoes are the type you should plant. Try a few plants of Burpee's Longkeeper. These tomatoes can be harvested and left on a shelf to ripen well into the winter without spoiling.

Timed planting. Plan your vegetable garden, setting down approximate planting dates for various vegetables to stagger the harvest. This will prevent the problems that arise when everything is ready at the same time.

Research harvest recipes. Go through your recipe files and cookbooks to find your favorite summertime recipes, especially those using vegetables that you will be preserving. Add new ones that you would like to try. Aim for easy, quick-to-prepare foods. Put these recipes in a special file.

Collect preserving recipes. Collect recipes for sauces, jams, jellies, preserves, pickles, and relishes (see recipe section for more). Put these recipes together in your special summertime file or create a new one for them.

Stock up on supplies. Once you have decided which recipes you would like to try, calculate how much sugar, pickling salt, spices, vinegar, and freezer bags you will need, and buy a little each time you shop. This will save extra shopping trips at your busiest time and spread the cost of the extras over a longer period of time.

Jar storage. Clear at least one large shelf in a clean, enclosed area (kitchen cupboard, nearby closet, or pantry) to store canning jars that can be washed ahead of time.

Early Spring through Early Summer

Meals ahead. As winter slips into early spring, prepare extra meals to tuck away in the freezer for harvest day dinners without effort.

Sewing for harvest time. Make little muslin herb and spice bags, food straining bags, heavy potholders, and cover-all aprons. These aprons save on laundry and can be made easily from old shirts. Just remove the collars and sleeves and finish off the rough edges with binding tape. For the little ones, make large bibs out of old flannel-backed plastic table-cloths and a little bias tape.

Recycled strainers. Old stockings and panty hose make handy food strainers. Cut the crotch and legs out of clean, old panty hose, tie or sew one end, and use them for extra straining bags.

Examine canning jars. Check your canning jars for nicks and cracks; discard those unsafe for food storage.

Locate markets. To save time in late summer, locate farmers' markets or truck gardens in your area in the late spring or early summer. Vegetables and fruits from these sources can supplement your own garden produce.

Spring cleaning. As your root cellar empties in the spring, clean all shelves well to avoid insect and bacteria problems during the warmer months.

Defrost the freezer. Defrost and clean your freezer late in the spring. (Use a blower-type hair dryer to hasten the defrosting.) Remove all frozen foods from plastic containers and refreeze the food in marked plastic bags. The foods will come out of the plastic containers easily if you run a little hot water over the bottom and sides. Wash containers in warm, sudsy water containing baking soda to get rid of unwanted odors. Throw away all foods that are past their prime, or use them as soon as possible in soups, stews, or casseroles. Those that must be discarded should go out to the pigs or to the compost pile.

Oil sprays. Spray the walls and bottom of the cleaned freezer with a vegetable oil spray to make future clean-ups easier.

Prepare temporary cold storage. Scrub out any extra garbage cans you have, or buy a new one. In the height of the harvest season, you can fill these cans with ice and produce to keep your vegetables fresh and chilled.

Cut freezer costs. To save on the cost of running your freezer, fill it with ice packs (see chapter 3, page 29) or milk cartons of water as it empties. A full freezer costs less to run, and the ice will come in handy to cool blanched vegetables.

Preseason workshops. Get together with a group of friends and encourage local stores and Cooperative Extension Services to give food preservation classes in the late spring prior to the harvest season, rather than during harvest season when you are too busy to attend.

CHAPTER 3

The Basic Techniques of Root Cellaring, Freezing, Drying, and Canning

THE EASIEST, FASTEST, OLDEST METHOD of food preservation is root cellaring, or cold storage. The problems with this method are that many fruits and vegetables do not adapt well to cold storage, and many homes do not have root cellars.

The second fastest and easiest method of food preservation is freezing. But, not all fruits and vegetables freeze well, and many people don't own freezers.

Dehydrating, or drying, foods is an ancient method of food preservation. It requires little in the way of preparation, compared to freezing and canning. And although the process is time-consuming, you are free to be elsewhere while the dehydrator, your oven, or the sun does the work. Dried foods are easy to store and have a long shelf life. Drying intensifies the flavors of foods, which can be good or bad, depending on your point of view. Not all foods lend themselves to drying.

Canning is probably the most time-consuming method of food preservation, but sometimes it gives the very best product. So, instead of ignoring canning altogether, I will show you ways of saving time when canning — so that you can have the very best home-preserved foods.

The key to saving time when processing food is to be very organized

— to have all your equipment ready and to have your tasks sorted out (and, even better, shared with other members of the family). So here is a step-by-step method for each food preservation technique. Take the time to study the method carefully; then turn to the sections on the individual vegetables and fruits for more details, and follow those brief steps to process the fruits and vegetables you have on hand with the method that is best for you.

Root Cellaring

If you are one of the lucky people who has a storage area that will keep foods cool without freezing them, you can store some fruits (apples, grapefruit, grapes, and pears) and vegetables (shell beans, beets, cabbages, carrots, cauliflower, celery, kohlrabi, onions, peppers, potatoes, pumpkins, winter squash, and green tomatoes) without processing. Or you can temporarily store these vegetables until the rush of the harvest season and the winter holidays is over. With more space in your freezer and many canning jars emptied, you can process apples, beets, carrots, cauliflower, pumpkins, and tomatoes at your leisure.

Clean out cellar.

Storing in a Root Cellar: 6 Easy Steps

1. Clean your root cellar or storage area once a year, just before the harvest season. Sweep out the area, scrub all your containers, and leave the area open to air for a few days.

2. Assemble your containers. Since different fruits and vegetables have different storage requirements — some like it cool and dry, some like it cool and moist — you will need to provide different conditions. Onions, pumpkins, and squash need dry conditions with plenty of air circulation. Root vegetables like it moist; store them in sturdy boxes, barrels, large plastic bags, or crocks. Packing fruits and vegetables in layers of dried leaves,

Assemble containers.

straw, or crumpled newspapers will
help absorb excess odors.

3. Harvest the best produce.
Remove any injured or overripe
produce and use immediately.

4. Season each vegetable as
needed. For winter squash and
pumpkins, this means leaving
them to dry in the sun. Onions
should be dried before storing.
Read under the individual vegetables for specifics.

5. Pack the unwashed fruits and
vegetables in suitable containers.

Pack in containers.

6. Check your stored foods from time to time. Remove any that are
beginning to soften or show signs of spoiling. If possible, use immediately or freeze or can.

Freezing

Freezing maintains the natural color, fresh flavor, and high nutritive value
of fresh foods. When properly frozen, fruits and vegetables are more like
fresh than when processed by any other method of food preservation.
Best of all, freezing is fast and easy.

After I had been freezing garden surpluses for years, I discovered that
the old standard method of freezing (washing and preparing the vegetables,
then blanching, cooling, drying, packing, and freezing them) was not the
fastest, easiest way to produce the best finished product. After all, you
would not use the same recipe to cook every vegetable, would you? So I
experimented with new ways of freezing and have had excellent results.
Many vegetables can be frozen without blanching (although their shelf
lives in the freezer will be shorter). Greens can be stir-fried instead of
blanched for a better product. I'll go over each method step-by-step, but
first, a few words about organizing your work and getting your packaging
materials ready.

Packaging Frozen Foods

Proper packaging is absolutely necessary to prevent freezer burn,
oxidation, and formation of large ice crystals.

For freezing most of the vegetables in this book, I strongly recommend using *boilable bags*. These are heavy-duty freezer bags that allow
you to blanch, cool, freeze, then cook your vegetables right in the bag.

They are sealed with an automatic sealer or your own electric flat iron.

Other freezer packaging materials you can use are freezer paper, heavy foil, wide-mouth freezer jars with straight sides (for easy removal of frozen foods), rigid plastic containers, and plastic freezer bags. Square freezer jars or rigid containers make better use of freezer space than round ones. If you don't use boilable bags, use only heavy-duty plastic bags that are labeled *food safe*.

It is important to remove as much air as possible from packages of food before freezing. Excess air in the packages causes oxidation, which lowers the quality of the food, and vacuum-packed bags take up less freezer space.

There are accessories on the market for removing air from plastic bags, but you can remove as much air as these appliances do, without investing any money, by pressing the air out with a pillow or your hand. This method works best with boilable bags.

Partially seal.

1. Fill the bag with vegetables and distribute the vegetables evenly in the bag.

2. With a small pillow or your hand, press down gently, but firmly, on the bag to expel all the air you can.

3. Hold the bag closed between your thumb and forefinger. Press the sealing bar down and hold a few seconds longer than recommended. Move the bag ½ inch and seal again.

If you don't have an automatic bag sealer, use an electric flat iron, as follows:

Remove the air.

1. Place a filled bag on a heavy towel, and place a damp cotton cloth over the edge of the bag.

2. Partially seal the bag with an iron, leaving 1½ inches open.

3. Remove the air by pressing a small pillow or your hand on the bag, gently but firmly.

4. Finish sealing with the electric iron over the damp cotton cloth.

> *TIP* To prevent injury *when slicing vegetables with a manually operated rotary slicer, blade slicer, or slaw slicer, wear a clean cotton garden glove on the hand that is apt to come in contact with the slicing blade.*

Complete seal.

Washing Vegetables and Fruit

Wash your vegetables and fruit in plenty of water. Use a medium-stiff bristled brush or a plastic or nylon net scrubber that can get into crevices where the dirt is hardest to remove. Be especially thorough with root crops, since botulism bacteria may be in the soil and only thorough washing will remove them.

Always lift produce out of the water rather than letting the water drain off. Drain vegetables on absorbent toweling, patting as dry as possible.

Reusable Ice Packs: A Big Time-Saver

It's worth investing in a box of quart-size boilable freezer bags to make ice packs for freezing. Use those bags, instead of cubes or chunks of ice, to quick-chill blanched food (see pages 36 and 38). When you are through freezing for the day, remove the bags from the water, wipe them dry with a towel, and return them to the freezer to refreeze. This saves the fuss of making ice cubes and the frustration of running out of ice in the middle of a large freezing project, and the bags of ice last much longer than either ice cubes or chunks of ice. Here's how you can make these ice packs.

Fill bag with water.

1. Fill boilable freezer bags ¾ full of cold water.

2. Hold the bag over the edge of your shelf or counter.

3. Seal with electric sealer, or

Seal with electric sealer.

place the bag on a heavy towel, cover with a damp cloth, and press with a hot iron. Freeze.

TIP *All vegetables that are blanched can be tray-frozen, then bagged. This allows you to postpone packaging until the next day, when you may have more time. Also, it makes it possible to package vegetables loosely in large bags or containers. When you want some vegetables, they will pour freely from the bag.*

TIP *Frozen, unblanched vegetables are best cooked by stir-frying. To do so, melt 1 teaspoon of butter per serving in a heavy, preheated skillet. When the butter has melted, add the frozen vegetables and stir and toss the vegetables over high heat to the desired degree of tenderness. Cook until all moisture is evaporated. If more moisture is needed to cook to desired stage of doneness, add water, 1 tablespoon at a time.*

TIP *Tray-frozen fruits and vegetables should be packaged as soon as possible, but if you are short on time, slip a large, food-safe plastic bag over the tray and tie it closed. Package as soon as you have a chance. Do not leave trays in bags longer than 24 hours.*

Unblanched Freezing: 5 Quick Steps

This is the fastest, easiest method of freezing. It was originally thought that this method was acceptable only for chopped onions, peppers, fresh herbs, or other vegetables that were to be stored for less than 1 month. But I have found that many unblanched, frozen vegetables can be stored for much longer and still maintain good color, flavor, and texture. Try this method with onions, peppers, herbs, celery, corn in husks, cabbage, Sugar Snap peas, summer squash, young, tender broccoli, and green and yellow beans. It is the preferred method to use with berries. It can also be used with super-quality fruits, especially ones you plan to use semi-thawed or baked in a dessert, such as a crisp or a crumble.

1. Make sure your work area and all equipment are spotlessly clean. Assemble your equipment and set your tools where they will be most useful. You will need a scrubbing brush, 2 or 3 heavy bath towels, freezer bags and small pillow (optional), and a labeling pen and tape.

2. Select vegetables that are slightly *immature*. Wash the vegetables and drain on absorbent toweling.

3. Prepare the vegetables: slice, dice, chop, julienne, or leave whole. Leave berries whole; peel and slice or chop other fruit.

4. Pack in freezer bags, expelling as much air as possible. Label with name of product and date.

5. Freeze in a single layer in the coldest part of the freezer.

Vegetables and fruits frozen this way should be used within 3 months. The best methods of cooking vegetables frozen in this manner are stir-frying and steaming.

TIP *The more accessible the proper tools for food processing are, the faster, easier, and more enjoyable the job will be. After using large appliances, such as food processors, I always wash and set them back up again. I cover my strainer with a plastic bag to prevent dirt and bacteria from collecting in the open funnel top.*

Drain washed beans.

Julienne beans.

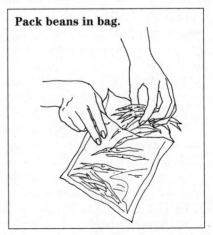
Pack beans in bag.

Boilable Freezer Bag Method: 12 Steps

This method of freezing often produces the best-tasting vegetables. Since the vegetables never come in contact with water, all color, flavor, texture, and most nutrients are preserved. Adding butter to the bag, when desired, coats the vegetables with a protective film that further enhances the quality and flavor of the finished product. Experiment with combinations of vegetables, such as peas and tiny onions, or peas and carrots. Sliced, diced, or julienne vegetables work best. Whole carrots and beets do not freeze well by this method. Strong-flavored vegetables, such as broccoli, cauliflower, cabbage, and turnips, should not be frozen by this method.

Time is saved with this method because bags of food can be blanched in multiples; cooling requires no special timing or handling (allowing you to continue packing); and since all vegetables are processed within the package, pans need only to be rinsed and dried, making clean-up a snap.

I tested this method against the standard freezing method with green beans. After the initial washing and trimming (time for both was the same), I timed the balance of the freezing procedure. I was able to pack, blanch, and cool ½ bushel of green beans by the boilable freezer bag method in 29 minutes, versus 1 hour and 25 minutes for the standard method. Try it yourself!

The real challenge with this method is locating a bag sealer and suitable freezer bags. If you can't find a source locally, check the mail-order listings on page 198.

1. Make sure your work area and all equipment are spotlessly clean. Assemble your equipment and set your tools where they will be most useful. You will need a scrub brush, heavy bath towels, chopping board, knives, food processor, wide-mouth funnel or large spoon, freezer bags, small pillow (optional), bag sealer or electric flat iron, indelible marking pen and freezer tape, large roaster half-filled with water for blanching, large kettle for cooling, ice packs, cubes, or chunks of ice, tongs, potholders, and a timer.

2. Select young, fresh vegetables that are just table-ready or slightly immature. Wash well, drain on absorbent toweling.

3. Begin heating water in the roaster for blanching.

4. Prepare vegetables as desired: slice, dice, chop, julienne, or leave whole (except for large, dense vegetables, such as carrots and beets).

5. Plug in bag sealer or iron. Fill 4 boilable bags with vegetables in meal-size portions, making sure that when the vegetables are distributed, the package is no thicker than 1 inch. Add butter and seasonings if desired. Use as much as you would use if cooking for a meal.

6. Expel as much air as possible and seal with an automatic bag sealer.

Or place the bag in a heavy bath towel, cover with a damp cloth, and seal with an electric iron. Label and date bag.

7. When 4 bags are packed, drop them into the boiling water and blanch with the pan covered. (The bags will float on top of the water. This is all right, as long as each bag has one side in contact with the boiling water.) Check the timing and set the timer. A rule of thumb is to blanch for double the length of time suggested for the standard blanching method. Use a slightly shorter time for tender young vegetables, and a slightly longer time for more mature ones. Start counting the time as soon as you replace the cover.

8. Fill the cooling kettle with cold water and ice packs (see page 29) or cubes or chunks of ice.

Continue packing while the first batch is blanching.

9. When the blanching time is up, remove the packages from the blanching kettle and place them in the ice water. Make sure the ice holds the bags down in the water, since air left in the bag tends to make the bags float. During the chilling time, occasionally knead the bags to move the cold into the center of the packages.

10. Add 4 more bags to the blancher and continue as before, until all the vegetables are blanched. Leave the processed bags in the ice until you are completely finished, unless you need the space for more vegetables.

When all the vegetables have been blanched, leave the bags in the

Pare produce.

Slice produce.

Fill meal-size bags.

ice water for an additional 10 minutes. While the bags are cooling, clean up your work area.

11. Remove the bags from the water and dry with absorbent towels.

12. Freeze the vegetables in a single layer in the coldest part of the freezer. Remove the ice bags from the cooling kettle, pat dry, and return to the freezer.

Foods frozen this way can be cooked in the bag or removed and steamed or stir-fried for faster cooking.

TIP *Instead of blanching your favorite vegetables, try stir-frying them in a little butter for a few minutes. Then package the vegetables in boilable bags. To prepare these vegetables for the table, reheat the bagged vegetables in boiling water. You will enjoy the stir-fry flavor and texture.*

TIP *When pouring large quantities of boiling water into the sink, run the cold water. This will prevent the steam from scalding you.*

TIP *To save confusion and mistakes when working with seasonings, always work from the right to left or vice-versa. As you use a seasoning, move it to the other side.*

Microwave Blanching Method for Freezing: 9 Steps

This method of freezing often produces great-tasting vegetables. Since the vegetables are not immersed in water, all color, flavor, texture, and most nutrients are preserved. Adding butter to the vegetables coats them with a protective film that further enhances the quality and flavor of the finished product. Experiment with combinations of vegetables, such as peas and tiny onions, or peas and carrots. Sliced, diced, or julienned vegetables work best. To promote even cooking, most vegetables require stirring halfway through the blanching process.

Please note: Microwave blanching for the freezer is not a tried-and-true method. Your local County Extension Service agent won't recommend it, as research has shown that all enzymes may not be destroyed by this method. This probably relates to the differing efficiencies of various microwave models, plus how evenly the vegetables were placed in the blanching container and whether or not the vegetables were stirred halfway through the blanching time. Note, too, that the individual blanching times per pound of vegetable are about the same as for blanching vegetables on top of the stove, plus you have to add stirring time. However, there is no time wasted while you wait for the water to return to a boil on top of the stove — and that is where the time-savings come in.

1. Make sure your work area and all equipment are spotlessly clean. Assemble your equipment and set your tools where they will be most useful. You will need a scrub brush, colander, strainers, paring and chopping knives, cutting board, food processor (optional), measuring cups, tongs, heavy towels, wax-paper-lined cookie sheets, freezer containers or bags, freezer tape and indelible marking pen, large microwave-safe container with lid or microwave-safe plastic wrap, potholders, and a timer.

2. Select young, fresh vegetables that are just table-ready or slightly immature. Wash, and drain on absorbent towels.

3. Prepare the vegetables as desired: slice, dice, chop, julienne, puree, or leave whole.

4. Clean the sink and fill with water and ice packs (see page 29) or cubes or chuncks of ice.

5. Blanch the vegetables. Work in 3- to 4-cup batches (1 to 1½ pounds). Arrange the vegetables in a large, shallow microwave-safe container and add ¼ to ½ cup water. Set the timer and blanch. Specific amounts for vegetables and water, as well as specific times, can be found for each vegetable on the chart found on page 195.

6. Cool the vegetables quickly in ice water. Cooling time is approximately the same as blanching.

7. Drain the vegetables thoroughly, removing as much water as possible by lifting them from the ice water onto heavy bath towels and patting them dry with another towel. While one batch of vegetables is chilling, pack any previously drained batches, and blanch another.

8. Place cooled, drained vegetables on wax-paper-lined cookie sheets and freeze until solid. Then package loosely in plastic bags that have been labeled with the date and product. Be sure to remove as much air as possible. You can package these vegetables in large bags and remove just the number of servings needed at a time.

You can also package the vegetables in freezer containers or freezer bags.

9. Freeze vegetables in a single layer in the coldest part of the freezer. Clean up when all vegetables are in the freezer. Wipe ice packs dry and return to the freezer.

Standard Freezing Method: 10 Steps

Pick up any book on food preservation written before the days of microwaves or boilable bags, or written without concern for saving time, and you will find this method. It works just fine and you get a very acceptable end product, but you will spend more time with it.

1. Make sure your work area and all equipment are spotlessly clean. Assemble your equipment and set your tools where they will be most useful. You will need a scrub brush, colander, strainers, paring and chopping knives, cutting board, food processing equipment (optional), measuring cups, tongs, heavy towels, wax-paper-lined cookie sheets, freezer containers or bags, freezer tape and indelible marking pen, blanching kettle half-filled with water, potholders, and a timer.

2. Select young, fresh vegetables that are just table-ready or slightly immature. Wash, and drain on absorbent towels.

3. Begin heating water in the blanching kettle.

4. Prepare the vegetables as desired: slice, dice, chop, julienne, puree, or leave whole.

5. Clean the sink and fill with water and ice packs (see page 29) or cubes or chunks of ice.

6. Blanch the vegetables. If you have a boiling water blancher, immerse the vegetables in boiling water, 1 pound at a time. Start counting as soon as the water returns to a boil, and blanch as long as the chart on page 196 indicates. If it takes longer than 2 minutes for the water to return to a boil, blanch fewer vegetables at a time.

If you have a steam blancher, blanch 1 pound of vegetables at a time in a steam basket or blancher suspended over boiling water, for the same length of time as for boil-

Drain produce on towel.

Blanch the produce.

Cool in ice water.

Drain produce on towel.

Freeze on cookie sheet.

Fill meal-size bags.

ing water. Start counting time as soon as you cover the pan. You can stack 3 blanchers to process up to 2½ pounds of vegetables at a time. Add 2 minutes to the blanching times, and begin counting time as soon as the pan is covered. It is a good idea to put the larger pieces of vegetables on the bottom and the smaller pieces at the top.

7. Cool the vegetables quickly in ice water. Cooling time is approximately the same as blanching. *Do not immerse the blanching utensil in the ice water* — this will warm the water unnecessarily, requiring more ice or a longer cooling time; and when you return the blancher to the boiling water, it will require more time and energy to return the blancher to the boiling point.

8. Drain the vegetables thoroughly, removing as much water as possible by lifting them from the ice water onto heavy bath towels and patting them dry with another towel. While one batch of vegetables is chilling, pack any previously drained batches, and blanch another.

9. Line cookie sheets with wax paper, place cooled, drained vegetables on sheets, and freeze until solid. Then package loosely in plastic bags that have been labeled with the date and product. Be sure to remove as much air as possible. You can package these vegetables in large bags and remove just the number of servings needed at a time.

You can also package the vegetables in freezer containers or freezer bags.

10. Freeze vegetables in a single layer in the coldest part of the freezer. Clean up when all vegetables are in the freezer. Wipe ice packs dry and return to the freezer.

Drying

Drying foods is a natural alternative for people with limited time and limited space for storing frozen or canned foods. Compared with canning, the process is much less complicated — and the only special equipment is a dehydrator, though it is possible to dry without one. Compared to freezing, it is less expensive and worry-free; power failures represent no threat to dried foods. Almost any food can be dried, but I will focus on the foods that are most popularly dried: fruits and a few vegetables, including mushrooms, and herbs.

To Pretreat or Not to Pretreat

Drying foods, like freezing, does not stop the enzymatic action that causes fruit to mature and eventually decay; it only slows it down. Some foods keep well without pretreatment, but others will continue to deteriorate in color, flavor, texture, and nutrients for months after they have dried unless they are treated. Pretreatment can mean blanching, as you would do before freezing vegetables, or dipping the food in ascorbic acid, fruit juice, salt water, or a commercial preparation that contains ascorbic acid or sodium sulfite. Specific pretreatment recommendations are found with each vegetable and fruit listing in chapters 4 and 5.

Blanching. If you have a boiling water blancher, immerse the vegetables in boiling water, 1 pound at a time. Start counting as soon as the water returns to a boil, and blanch as long as the chart on page 196 indicates. If it takes longer than 2 minutes for the water to return to a boil, blanch fewer vegetables at a time.

If you have a steam blancher, blanch 1 pound of vegetables at a time in a steam basket or blancher suspended over boiling water, for the same length of time as for boiling water. Start counting time as soon as you cover the pan. You can stack 3 blanchers to process up to 2½ pounds of vegetables at a time. Add 2 minutes to the blanching times, and begin counting time as soon as the pan is covered. It is a good idea to put the larger pieces of vegetables on the bottom and the smaller pieces at the top.

If you have a microwave, arrange 3 to 4 cups of vegetables in a container and add ¼ to ½ cup water. Set the timer and blanch.

Specific amounts for vegetables and water, as well as specific times, can be found for each vegetable on the chart found on page 198.

Cool the vegetables quickly in ice water. Cooling time is approximately the same as blanching. Drain the vegetables thoroughly, removing as much water as possible by lifting them from the ice water onto heavy bath towels and patting them dry with another towel.

Salt Water Dip. Dissolve 6 tablespoons flaked pickling salt in 1 gallon of lukewarm water. To keep fruit from darkening, slice or chop it directly into the water. Allow it to soak for no more than 5 minutes or the fruit will absorb too much water and acquire a salty taste. Drain before loading drying trays. *This is not recommended for those on a low-sodium diet.*

Ascorbic Acid Dip. Ascorbic acid is a form of vitamin C. Dissolve 2 tablespoons of ascorbic acid crystals, 2 tablespoons of ascorbic acid powder, or 5 crushed 1-gram vitamin C tablets in 1 quart of lukewarm water. Slice or chop fruits directly into the solution. When 1 or 2 cups of fruit have accumulated in the solution, give it a stir and remove the fruit with a slotted spoon. Drain well before loading drying trays.

Fruit Juice Dip. Dip peaches, apples, or banana slices into 1 quart undiluted pineapple juice or 1 quart lukewarm water into which ¼ cup lemon juice has been stirred. Let fruits remain in the dip for no more than 5 to 10 minutes. Drain well before drying.

Testing Dried Foods

Before dried foods are stored, they should be tested to be sure enough moisture has been removed to make it impossible for mold and bacteria to grow and cause decay. Well-dried foods will vary from a moisture content of 5 percent for leafy vegetables, such as spinach, to 25 percent for juicy acid fruits, such as apricots. You can judge the percent of moisture by weighing the food before and after drying. One pound of tomatoes before drying will weigh 4 ounces when properly dried to a moisture level of 25 percent.

All dried foods should be cooled before testing for drying because warm foods feel more moist than when they have cooled. In general, dried foods feel dry when they are squeezed.

Root vegetables, squash, and pumpkin are dry when they are tough and leathery, still pliable, but with no moisture in the center. Celery should be hard and brittle. To test, cut through the center with a knife or take a bite of it.

Green beans should be dark green and leathery. Greens, such as spinach, should be brittle enough to crumble in the hands. Corn, peas, and dry beans should be dry enough to shatter or split in half when tapped with a hammer.

Fruits are dry when leathery enough that several pieces will spring back without sticking together after being squeezed. Fruits such as peaches, pears, apples, and plums, should remain pliable. Berries, rhubarb, and lemon or orange peel should be crisp and brittle. Banana slices may be crisp or slightly pliable, depending on the thickness of the slices and the method of pretreatment.

Fruit leathers are still slightly sticky to the touch when they are dried, but will pull away from the plastic wrap easily. For long-term storage, dry leathers until they are no longer sticky.

Herb leaves are dry enough for storage when they are so brittle they will crumble easily in your hands.

TIP *Leathers have almost as many names as they have uses. The first settlers in the Old West made leathers to preserve the goodness of fruits and vegetables that would otherwise have gone to waste. They called them "papers" because of their paper-thinness, or "fruit leathers" because of their pliable, leathery texture. Today they may be called fruit rolls or fruit taffy because of their delicious, candy-like taste.*

Storing Dried Foods

Dried foods should be stored in small batches in airtight, insect-proof containers — glass or plastic jars or zipper-lock plastic bags.

After the dried food has cooled, place it in a storage container and seal tightly. Don't delay this step, or the dried produce will begin to accumulate moisture. Watch for signs of moisture inside the jars or bags. If moisture appears, either the food is not dry or the container was not properly sealed. If there are no signs of mold, return the food to the dehydrator for further drying. Molded foods should be thrown out.

Fruit leathers can be rolled in plastic wrap or waxed paper. Stand the rolls in a metal or glass container — clean, dry coffee cans work well — and seal with a tight-fitting lid.

Because their flavors are easily lost, herbs, herb mixtures, and herb teas are best stored separately in very small containers, such as clean, dry pill bottles or baby food jars. Be certain, though, that the bottles are odor-free. Herb leaves that are to be used within a few months usually are crumbled before storing, but, for the best flavor retention in long-term storage, store the leaves intact and crumble just before using.

Keep containers in a cool, dark, dry place.

TIP *Dried foods can make lovely gifts. Fill small baby food jars with dried herbs or herb mixtures. Paste pretty labels on the jars and include a few recipes on decorative file cards. Or package a mixed variety of fruit leather strips in plastic wrap and tie with a big ribbon.*

TIP   *There will be times when the weather is humid or your dryer is overloaded, or it just isn't convenient to dry foods at harvest time. Apples, pears, onions, celery, squash, pumpkins, and carrots can be stored in a cool, dry storage room for a few weeks, until you are ready to dry them. Green peppers, corn, peaches, and strawberries can be stored in the freezer until a more convenient time. Blanch corn and peaches as you would for freezer storage, but the other fruit and vegetables need no pretreatment. For fruit leathers, puree the fruit in a blender, pour into a container, and freeze. When you are ready to make the leathers, just thaw and spread the puree on drying trays.*

Drying Foods in a Dehydrator

You will get the most consistent results with a dehydrator. And, dehydrator drying is so trouble-free you can leave the dehydrator operating overnight or while you're away from home. Consider loading the dehydrator in the morning before you leave for work and letting it run all day. If a dryer load is almost dry at bedtime, just reduce the heat to 105° to 110°F and go to bed. By morning, the food will be ready to store.

1. Clean your work surface and assemble your tools. You will need knives, peelers, a cutting board, measuring cups and spoons and a bowl (if you are pretreating), a colander, and a heavy towel. Dehydrators come complete with their own trays.

2. Select young, fresh vegetables that are just table-ready or slightly immature. Select firm, ripe fruit. Wash, and drain on absorbent towels.

3. Preheat the dehydrator to the desired temperature. Recommended temperatures are 115°F for uncooked fruits, 120°F for vegetables and some cooked fruits, and 110°F for leafy herbs.

4. Peel, slice, dice, chop, julienne, halve, or leave whole, depending on the recommendations for the specific fruit, vegetable, or herb. Pretreat or blanch according to the recommendations for each food.

5. Spread the prepared foods evenly over the dehydrator trays in thin layers. Different foods can be dried at the same time, but very moist foods should not be dried with almost-dry foods, nor should you combine foods with strong odors or flavors.

6. Dry according to the times specified for each food. Test for dryness according to the recommendations on page 40. Rotate the trays front to back, side to side, and top to bottom at least once during the drying process. Also stir the food or turn it.

7. Package dried foods in airtight bottles, jars, or plastic bags. Store in a cool, dark place.

Drying Food in a Conventional Oven

Drying food in an oven is sometimes better than sun drying, because it is possible to have controlled, even temperatures, but it has the disadvantage of poor air circulation, and air movement is necessary for even drying. Air circulation can be improved by leaving the oven door ajar a few inches and placing an electric fan in front of the door, positioning it to blow away moist air as it accumulates.

Although commercial drying trays are available for use in an oven, homemade trays can be made of wooden frames and nylon screening. For air circulation, allow 1 inch space on each side, 3 inches on top and bottom, and 2½ inches between trays.

1. Clean your work surface and assemble your tools. You will need knives, peelers, a cutting board, measuring cups and spoons and a bowl (if you are pretreating), a colander, a heavy towel, and storage containers. You will also need a thermometer that registers from 100°F to 150°F.

2. Select young, fresh vegetables that are just table-ready or slightly immature. Select firm, ripe fruit. Wash, and drain on absorbent towels.

3. Set a large, easily read thermometer on the top shelf of the oven and preheat to the desired temperature. Recommended temperatures are 115°F for uncooked fruits, 120°F for vegetables and some cooked fruits, and 110°F for leafy herbs.

4. Peel, slice, dice, chop, julienne, halve, or leave whole, depending on the recommendations for the specific fruit, vegetable, or herb. Pretreat or blanch according to the recommendations for each food.

5. Spread the prepared foods sparsely but evenly over the dehydrator trays in thin layers. Different foods can be dried at the same time, but very moist foods should not be dried with almost-dry foods, nor should you combine foods with strong odors or flavors.

6. Place the trays in the oven, leaving the door ajar. Set an electric fan in front of the door. Dry according to the directions for each food, stirring or turning the food occasionally and rotating the trays front to back, side to side, and top to bottom every 2 to 3 hours.

7. Package dried foods in airtight bottles, jars, or plastic bags. Store in a cool, dark place.

Sun-Drying

If you are blessed with clean air, low humidity, and an abundance of hot, sunny days, sun-drying is the least expensive and simplest method of preserving foods. But, drying outdoors is unpredictable unless the temperatures are over 100°F, and the relative humidity is low. If the temperature is too low, the humidity is too high, or both, spoilage will occur before drying is achieved. Because sun-drying is slower and food is exposed for a longer period of time, pretreating is more important than for drying in a dehydrator.

1. Clean your work surface and assemble your tools. You will need knives, peelers, a cutting board, measuring cups and spoons (for pretreating), a colander, a heavy towel, and storage containers. You will also need a cheesecloth for protecting food from insects and birds. Drying trays can be cookie sheets or homemade wooden trays, but drying is speeded if air is allowed to circulate freely, so trays made of fiberglass or stainless steel screening work best. *Do not use galvanized screen, which will contaminate food.*

2. Select young, fresh vegetables that are just table-ready or slightly immature. Select firm, ripe fruit. Wash, and drain on absorbent towels.

3. Peel, slice, dice, chop, julienne, halve, or leave whole, depending on the recommendations for the specific fruit, vegetable, or herb. Pretreat or blanch according to the recommendations for each food.

4. Spread the prepared foods sparsely but evenly over the dehydrator trays in thin layers. Different foods can be dried at the same time. Cover with cheesecloth.

5. Place the trays in a well-ventilated spot in full sun. Every few hours, turn or stir the food. Take trays inside at night. (Do not include inside time when calculating drying time.)

6. Before storing, place food in oven set at 125°F for 30 minutes to kill any insect eggs that may have been deposited on them, or place in the freezer for a day or two. Then package in airtight bottles, jars, or plastic bags. Store in a cool, dark place.

Making Fruit Leathers

Any fruit (or vegetable) or combination of fruits can be made into leathers. Leathers are an excellent way to use slightly overripe fruits, which have more flavor than just-ripe fruit anyway. Leathers can be made from purees of raw or cooked fruits. You can add water or juice to the blender to get a mixture thin enough to pour. Figure that 2 cups of puree will fill a standard 10-inch by 15-inch cookie sheet.

1. Strain cooked or thoroughly ripened raw fruit through a food mill or liquefy in a blender until you have a smooth puree. If needed, add juice or water to make the mixture thin enough to pour.

2. Line a drying tray with plastic wrap (or use the fruit leather sheet that came with your dehydrator). Spread the puree ⅛-inch thick on the drying tray.

3. *To dry in a dehydrator* set tray in dehydrator at 120°F for 6 to 8 hours, or until leather can be pulled easily from plastic. Invert, pull off plastic, and continue drying for another 4 to 6 hours. *To dry in a conventional oven*, put tray in oven at 120°F for 6 to 8 hours or until leather can be pulled easily from plastic. Invert, pull off plastic, and continue drying for another 6 to 8 hours. *To dry in the sun*, set tray outdoors for 1 day, or until leather can be pulled easily from plastic. Invert, pull off plastic, and dry for 1 more day.

4. To store, roll up in waxed paper or plastic wrap, close and twist ends and store in the refrigerator for up to 6 weeks.

Canning

Does a busy person can? Some of us do. Canning sounds old-fashioned, laborious, and difficult. In fact, although it is more time-consuming than freezing, and more labor-intensive than root cellaring or drying, it is not difficult. Also, nothing beats the convenience of having canned tomatoes ready to turn into an instant sauce, or opening a jar of applesauce or sugar-free peaches as an instant snack for hungry kids. If you are planning to

Two-piece screw band and lid.

make pickles, jams, or salsas, you will find that canning is necessary for the best finished product. So while you may not need to know how to can to preserve most vegetables, having the technique in your repetoire will give you the most variety in your pantry.

In this book I focus on boiling water bath canning, limited to high-acid fruits and vegetables and pickles, and pressure canning, the only acceptable method for low-acid vegetables. I will also show you two methods of packing jars — hot pack and cold pack. If you are interested in pressure canning, consult your local Extension Service agent or one of the books listed in the section of suggested reading.

Canning Jars and Lids

Use only ½-pint, pint, 1½-pint, and quart jars made especially for canning. Commercial jars, such as the type mayonnaise comes in, are too thin and will not withstand the heat required for processing vegetables. European-made jars cannot be used with our time charts because they are calibrated in metric sizes. Make sure your jars are free from nicks and cracks.

Although you can still find old-fashioned lids at garage sales, the modern 2-piece screw band and lid is the type of lid you will most likely work with, and it is the safest. These must be used with threaded jars. The metal lids have a flanged edge with a rubberlike sealing compound on their edges which seals to the edge of the jar. The lid is held in place with a screw band during processing. After the jars have been sealed, the screw band should be removed. The band can be reused to process other jars, but the lids are not reusable.

Preparing Jars and Lids

Wash enough jars for several batches of food all at once. A dishwasher comes in handy for this job. Place the jars upside down on clean towels in a clean area. They will be ready when you have time to can.

If your jars have not been prewashed, wash and rinse them when you are setting up. Check for chips and cracks that might have occurred while you were washing.

To heat jars and keep them hot for canning, fill a roasting pan with water, set in the oven at 200°F and leave the jars in the water until you need them. You can also heat jars by keeping them in the dishwasher on the dry cycle. Jars that are filled with food and processed for less than 10 minutes, as for jams and jellies, must be sterilized by boiling in the boiling water bath for 10 minutes before filling.

Place jar lids and screw bands in water according to the manufacturer's directions.

Tips on Washing Vegetables

Wash vegetables in plenty of cold water. Use a medium-stiff bristled brush or a plastic or nylon net scrubber that can get into the crevices where the dirt is hardest to remove. A stiff-bristled brush will just skim over these areas. Be especially thorough with root crops since botulism bacteria may be in the soil, and only thorough washing will remove them from the vegetables. Always lift vegetables out of the water rather than letting water drain off; otherwise the dirt will be redeposited on them.

Raw-Pack Versus Hot-Pack

Raw-Pack. Raw-pack is sometimes referred to as cold-pack — it means packing prepared vegetables and fruit into the canning jar raw. This is the fastest method of packing since it does not require heated jars or precooked food. Clean-up is faster because you do not have the extra pans and utensils to wash.

Any disadvantages to raw-packing? There will be some shrinkage, and occasionally the fruits or vegetables will float to the top of the jar (especially tomatoes). The jars will hold slightly less when packed this way. Also, the entrapped air may cause discoloration of the food after two to three months of storage. But I don't think these drawbacks outweigh the ease of preparation and the time savings of this method.

Hot-Pack. To hot-pack a jar, precook your food in simmering water, juice, or syrup for about 5 minutes; then pack the hot foods loosely into hot jars. Obviously, this method is more time consuming than the raw-pack method.

Sealing Jars

With the modern 2-piece screw bands and lids, you will have to buy new lids each time you process. Follow the manufacturer's directions for sealing.

When processing time is completed, remove the jars from the canner and place them several inches apart on a heavy towel. Do not tighten screw bands on jars with the 2-piece screw band and lids.

Do not open any jar, even if liquid has boiled out. The food is safe as long as the jar seals properly.

Do not cover the jars while they are cooling. Allow the jars to cool for 24 hours; then test the seal.

TIP *Salt is added to canned vegetables for taste. It is not necessary for any other reason.*

Testing Seals

After the cooling period is completed, remove the screw bands on jars with the 2-piece lids to prevent them from rusting onto the jars and to help you detect broken seals.

What does a good seal look like? The lid should be depressed in the center, and if you pick the jar up by the edge of the lid, it will not come loose. With the jar tipped upside down, check for any leaks. If there are any leaks, or if the center of the jar lid pops back, refrigerate that jar to use within a few days, or reprocess.

To reprocess, clean the rim of the jar. Add liquid, if necessary, to maintain the proper head space,

Check for leaks.

Test seal.

and put on a new lid and screw band. Then reprocess as before, for the full length of time recommended.

TIP *Make use of leisure time by chopping and dicing vegetables while watching your favorite show on television. Make a 12-inch cutting board out of 1-inch pine to fit your lap, and put the diced vegetables in a large plastic bag as you dice or cut them. Divide them into smaller bags later, or tray-freeze and package in larger bags.*

Storing Jars

Store jars in a cool, dark place, where they will not freeze. Warm temperatures cause discoloration and taste changes, and could cause spoilage that would not otherwise occur. Freezing does not make food unsafe, unless the jar is cracked or the cap loosened; but some foods may soften in texture.

Before using a jar of home-canned food, check for signs of spoilage. Bulging or unsealed lids, spurting liquid, mold, malodorous contents, or a constant stream of tiny bubbles when the jar is turned upside down indicate spoilage. Some bubbles are normal; but if after the contents have settled, you can see a constant flow of tiny bubbles from around the lid of the jar, then you must discard the contents. Discard the food from any jars that look suspicious. Food from these jars should be discarded where humans or animals will not eat it. The jars can be reused. Wash them well with hot sudsy water and boil them for 15 minutes before using the jars again.

TIP *Acid foods, including all fruits, tomatoes (to which you added lemon juice or citric acid), rhubarb, sauerkraut, and pickled foods, can be safely processed in a boiling water bath. Low-acid foods include all vegetables, except tomatoes, and all other foods that do not fall into the acid group, such as meat. Low-acid foods must be processed in a pressure canner.*

TIP To remove a stuck screw band, wring out a cloth in hot water, then wrap it around the band for a minute or so to help loosen it.

TIP To prevent hard-water mineral stains on jars and build-up in canners, use ½ cup vinegar per canner-full of hard water.

Boiling Water Bath Canning: 14 Steps

Boiling water bath canning is the USDA's recommended way of canning acid foods — fruits, pickles, and acidified tomatoes. With a boiling water bath canner, you immerse jars of food in hot water to cover and begin counting the processing time once the water begins to boil. This usually takes 25 to 30 minutes, depending on whether you are processing quarts or pints.

1. Make sure your work area and all equipment are spotlessly clean. If your jars have not been prewashed, wash and rinse them. Check the jars for nicks and cracks. If you plan to hot pack, keep the jars hot in water.

Assemble your equipment and set your tools where they will be most convenient. You will need a scrub brush, colander and/or strainer, paring and chopping knives, cutting board, food processing equipment, measuring cups and spoons, bubble expeller (wooden chopsticks work well), wide-mouth funnel, large bowls, canning jars, boiling water bath canner, preserving kettle, tea kettle filled with hot water, canning lids and screw bands, large wooden and slotted spoons, soup ladle, jar lifter or tongs, timer, hot pads, mitts or heavy potholders, and heavy bath towels.

2. Fill your canner with about 4 inches of water for pints and 4½ inches for quarts. (These amounts are for a 20 to 21 quart canner.) Place the canner on the stove and begin heating. Heat extra water to boiling in a tea kettle.

3. Wash your jars in soapy water, rinse well, and then keep hot by placing the jars in the preheating canner or in a dishwasher. If processing for less than 10 minutes, as for jams and jellies, sterilize the

Heat filled canner.

Place lids in water.

Wash produce.

Pack jars.

jars by boiling for 10 minutes in the canner. Leave the jars in the water until you are ready to process.

4. Place the jar lids and screw bands in water according to the manufacturer's directions.

5. Select perfect fruits and vegetables at the peak of their maturity. Wash the produce. Drain.

6. Prepare the vegetables: peel, slice, dice, julienne, leave whole, or puree.

7. Pack the jars.

Raw-pack. Firmly pack clean, heated jars with fruits or vegetables. If desired, add ½ teaspoon salt to pints, 1 teaspoon to quarts. Fill the jars with hot, not boiling, water, syrup, or juice, leaving the proper head space.

Hot-pack. Place prepared tomatoes, fruit, puree, or juice in a large pan; cover fruit with syrup or juice. Bring to a boil and simmer tomato products for 5 minutes, fruit for 3 minutes. Pack loosely into clean, hot jars, adding ½ teaspoon salt to pints and 1 teaspoon to quarts, if desired. Fill jars of whole tomatoes or fruit with hot liquid, leaving the recommended head space.

7. Expel air bubbles in the jar by running a nonmetallic kitchen utensil gently between vegetables and jar. Add more water if necessary to maintain the proper head space.

8. Wipe the rim of the jar with a clean, damp cloth and seal.

9. When the jars are packed and the lids are in place, check the canner. For raw-pack jars, if the water is boiling, add 1 quart of cold wa-

Expel air bubbles.

Wipe rim.

Lower jar into canner.

Start timer.

Remove jars to heavy towel.

Check seal.

ter to reduce the temperature enough to cushion the shock of adding the cooler jars to the boiling water.

Carefully lower the jars, using long-handled tongs or a jar lifter, into the hot water in the canner. Be careful not to bump jars against one another as you lower the rack; this could cause jars to crack. Water should cover jars by 2 full inches. If necessary, add more boiling water to the canner.

10. Start counting the processing time as soon as the water returns to a full boil. Keep the water at a full boil throughout the processing time. (A tea kettle of boiling water should be on hand to replenish the water in the canner, if necessary.)

11. If you are canning more than one batch of food, prepare the second batch while the first is processing. While the last batch is processing, clean your work area.

12. When processing time is up, carefully remove the cover from the canner. Using long-handled tongs or jar lifters, *carefully* remove jars from the canner. Place the jars several inches apart on a heavy bath towel away from drafts.

If the screw bands are loose, do not tighten them.

13. Cool the jars for 24 hours. After the cooling period is completed, remove the screw bands and check the seals. Wipe the sealed jars with a clean, damp cloth. Then label clearly with the product and date.

14. Store the jars in a cool, dark, dry place where they will not freeze.

TIP *If you do not have a dishwasher, a large kettle of hot, sudsy water will soak dishes out of the way of the work area, making clean-up chores easier when the sink is free.*

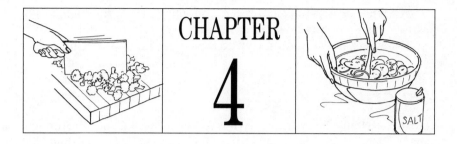

CHAPTER

4

Preserving Each Vegetable

THERE IS A BEST WAY TO PRESERVE each vegetable; there is a *fastest* way as well — and sometimes the best way is the fastest way, but not always. The best way means that the vegetable will taste closest to fresh when you cook it for the table.

Suppose your beans are ready to harvest. Turn to the page on beans in this chapter. Decide which preservation method to use. Does it look like you will have enough time to get the job done? Fine. Then read the harvest tips for beans, and go into the garden and pick the beans. What if you don't have enough time to process the beans? Those beans are going to get too mature out in the garden. You don't want to wait to pick them. In chapter 2, I shared some of the different shortcuts I have used in my kitchen — such as storing fresh vegetables overnight in garbage cans filled with ice, or tray-freezing unblanched beans to be used later in relishes. Check the index or skim through chapter 2 to find shortcuts that will work for you.

Please review the basic techniques. Before you start freezing, drying, or canning turn back to chapter 3 for a quick review of the basic techniques. Assembling all your equipment, setting up a productive work flow, and ensuring the safety of your methods will help to save you time in the long run.

With the basic techniques fresh in your mind, follow the step-by-step instructions I have provided for each vegetable.

Ready to harvest? Let's start with asparagus.

Asparagus

Asparagus should be picked when it is 6 to 8 inches high and thicker than a pencil. During harvesting, all shoots should be cut. Leaving the smaller shoots to grow will shorten the harvest season, which can continue for 6 to 10 weeks.

Freezing in Boilable Bags
Fast, Easy, Excellent Finished Product

1. Begin heating water for blanching. To prepare the asparagus, wash by scrubbing with a vegetable brush to remove any sand. Cut off tough ends or snap at the brittle point. Cut into pieces or sort spears. Pack in boilable bags.

Add butter and seasonings, if desired. Press out air. Seal bags.

2. Blanch bags, 4 at a time, in boiling water: 4 to 8 minutes, depending on size.

3. Cool. Pat bags dry. Freeze.

TIP *To cook vegetables frozen in boilable bags in the microwave, place the bag on a microwave-safe plate or bowl. Cut a ½-inch slit on the top side of the bag. Microwave on HIGH (100% power) for 4 to 6 minutes. Quarter-turn the dish halfway through the cooking, if necessary. Leave the vegetables in the bag for an additional 4 to 5 minutes, then serve.*

Freezing the Standard Way
More Time-Consuming, Finished Product Not as Good

1. Begin heating water for blanching in steamer. Scrub with a vegetable brush to remove any sand. Cut off tough ends or snap at the brittle point. Cut into pieces or sort spears.

2. Steam blanch, 1 pound at a time: 2 to 4 minutes depending on size.

3. Cool in ice water. Drain. Pack. Press out air. Seal. Freeze.

Beans: Green

The best beans for preserving are those that are slightly immature. Green beans should be long and slender and have tiny seeds. Harvest beans late in the day. The foliage should be dry. Harvesting beans from wet plants may cause the developing crop to rust.

Beans can be left to dry on the vine past maturity. After the pods are dry, shell them. Dry the beans on cookie sheets for several days. Place the beans in airtight containers and store in a dry place. These beans may be used as regular dried beans in soups and casseroles.

TIP *Another excellent way to preserve beans is to pickle them. You'll find a recipe for Dilly Beans on page 127.*

Can't preserve right away? Do not wash beans. Store by one of the methods suggested in chapter 3 (pages 27 to 39).

Freezing Unblanched Whole or Julienne Beans

Fastest, Best Finished Product

1. Trim ends of beans.

2. Wash, drain, pat thoroughly dry. Julienne, if desired.

3. Pack in gallon-size freezer bags. Press out air. Seal. Freeze.

Note: Unblanched beans will retain good quality for 6 months.

Trim bean ends.

Drain on towel.

Pack in freezer bags.

> *TIP* *Frozen beans should be cooked by steaming or stir-frying for best flavor and texture, or cooked in the boilable bag, for 18 to 20 minutes. The less contact beans have with water during freezing and cooking, the better flavor and texture they will have.*

Freezing in Boilable Bags
Fast, Easy, Excellent Finished Product

1. Begin heating water for blanching. To prepare the beans, trim the ends. Wash, drain, pat dry. Pack in boilable bags. Add butter and seasonings, if desired. Press out air. Seal bags.
2. Blanch bags, 4 at a time, in boiling water: 6 minutes for young beans, up to 8 minutes for old beans.
3. Cool. Pat bags dry. Freeze.

Freezing the Standard Way
More Time-Consuming, Finished Product Not as Good

1. Trim the ends from the beans. Begin heating water for blanching. Wash the beans, drain.
2. Steam-blanch, 1 pound at a time: 3 minutes for young beans, 4 minutes for old beans.
3. Cool in ice water. Drain. Pack. Press out air. Seal. Freeze.

Beets

Beets should be left in the garden until late fall. A few frosts will not harm them. Dig beets on a sunny day. Cut the tops off, leaving an inch of stem. Do not cut off roots. Let the beets lie on the ground until the following day. Beets stored in a root cellar will remain fresh and sweet-tasting well into late spring.

> *TIP* *Beets are good candidates for pickling. You'll find a recipe on page 126.*

TIP *Another method of peeling beets is to cut the tops from beets leaving 2 inches of stem to prevent bleeding. Do not cut the roots off. Scrub thoroughly. Place in a large kettle. Cover with hot tap water. Bring to a boil and boil for 15 to 20 minutes for canned beets, or until tender for frozen beets. Slip off skins. The disadvantage of this method is that beets should all be of the same size; otherwise, smaller beets will get overcooked and mushy before larger ones are cooked. This does not happen when beets are baked in the oven; beets of several sizes may be baked together and none overcook.*

Cold Storage

Fastest, Best Finished Product

1. Brush off the excess soil on the roots, but do not wash. Place a large plastic bag in a cardboard box; add 2 to 4 inches of *fresh* sawdust (2 inches for storage areas that will remain above freezing).

2. Add a single layer of beets, leaving a 2-inch space all around the side of the layer to be filled with sawdust. Cover with a 1-inch layer of sawdust. Continue to layer the beets until the box is full. Finish with a 2- to 4-inch layer of sawdust.

3. Fold over the top of the bag and close the box. Store in the coldest area of the root cellar or in an unheated area, such as a garage.

Brush soil off roots.

Layer beets in box.

Cover with sawdust.

Freezing Slices in Boilable Bags
Excellent Finished Product

1. Cut tops and roots off close to the beet. Preheat oven to 400°F. Scrub beets thoroughly. Place on a rack in a large roaster. Cover.
2. Bake until tender (approximately 1 hour for 2½ to 3-inch beets).
3. Fill the roaster with cold water to cool beets. Slip off skins.
4. Slice beets. Pack in boilable freezer bags. Add butter and seasoning, if desired. Press out air. Seal.
5. Cool in ice water. Wipe dry. Freeze.

Soak in salted water.

Broccoli

Harvest broccoli when the head stops growing, but before the individual clusters start to spread out. Second crop clusters (side shoots) should be cut while the buds are still clustered tightly.

Can't preserve right away? Do not wash. Store by one of the methods suggested in chapter 2.

TIP *When blanching broccoli, make long cross cuts in the stalk, so that the stalk will cook in the same length of time as the bud.*

Chop broccoli.

Freezing Unblanched Broccoli

Fastest Method, Good Finished Product

1. Soak broccoli in cold salted water for ½ hour to remove dirt and insects. Rinse well. Drain. Divide into uniform-size pieces or chop.
2. Pack in gallon-size freezer bags. Press out air. Seal. Freeze.

TIP *For best flavor and texture, frozen broccoli should be steamed or stir-fried.*

TIP *Unblanched broccoli florets retain good quality in the freezer for only 6 weeks, while the stalks hold up for 3 months. Save time by freezing sliced pieces of stalks without blanching, and blanch the florets for the best finished product. The sliced stalks make an excellent addition to mixed stir-fried vegetables.*

Pack into freezer bags.

Freezing the Standard Way
Best Finished Product

1. Soak broccoli in cold salted water for ½ hour to remove dirt and insects. Meanwhile, preheat water for steam blanching.

2. Drain broccoli. Rinse. Divide into uniform-size pieces or chop.

3. Steam blanch, 1 pound at a time for 5 minutes. Then, cool, drain, pack, press out air, and seal. Freeze.

Cabbage

Cabbage for winter keeping should be left in the garden as late in the fall as possible. Pick just before the first frost. If the heads indicate a tendency to split, and it's too early to harvest, give the heads a quarter turn to break off some of the roots; this will slow down the growth and can be repeated every 7 to 10 days. When ready to harvest, pull the entire plant up from the garden, roots and all.

Pull cabbage with roots.

Cold Storage
Fastest Method, Best Finished Product

1. Pull up cabbage plants with roots intact.

Hang to dry.

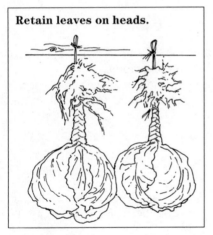

Retain leaves on heads.

2. Transfer freshly pulled cabbage plants directly to the root cellar, and hang upside down on hooks or nails.

3. Retain the outer leaves; they will form a dry paper-like covering that will help to keep the cabbage fresh.

TIP Finely shredded cabbage can be made into freezer coleslaw (page 125).

TIP Cabbage can be brined as sauerkraut or made into relishes; for recipes. See chapter 5.

TIP Outer leaves of cabbage can be frozen whole and unblanched to be used as wrappers for baked stuffed cabbage leaves. Since the leaves will wilt when defrosted, it will not be necessary to drop them into boiling water before preparing this dish.

TIP Coarsely chopped cabbage can be frozen unblanched to be used in soups or casserole dishes within 4 to 6 months. Steam-cook frozen cabbage for casserole dishes requiring cooked cabbage.

Carrots

Carrots should be left in the garden until you are ready to store or process them. Carrots for cold storage are best if harvested late in the fall, though they should not be allowed to become oversized and stringy. A few light frosts will not harm them. Carrots stored in a root cellar will remain fresh and sweet-tasting well into late spring.

Cold Storage
Fastest Method, Best Finished Product

1. Dig carrots on a sunny day; cut off tops close to the carrot and let them lie on the ground all day or even overnight to kill the little feeder roots. Do not wash the carrots.

2. Brush off excess soil. Place a large plastic bag in a cardboard box; add 2 to 4 inches of *fresh* sawdust (2 inches for storage areas that will remain above freezing). Add a single layer of carrots, leaving a 2-inch space all around the sides of the box to be filled with sawdust. Cover with a 1-inch layer of sawdust. Continue until box is full, finishing with a 2 to 4-inch layer of sawdust.

3. Fold over top of the bag and close the box. Store in the coldest area of the root cellar or an unheated area such as a garage.

Brush soil off carrots.

> *TIP* Mature fall carrots give a better finished frozen product than young early carrots. They should be peeled before freezing.

Layer carrots in box.

Freezing in Boilable Bags
Excellent Finished Product

1. Begin heating water for blanching. Scrub carrots thoroughly; peel. Slice or julienne with food processor.

2. Pack in boilable bags. Add butter and seasonings, if desired. Press out air. Seal.

Cover with sawdust.

3. Blanch bags (4 at a time) in boiling water, for 8 to 10 minutes.
4. Cool. Pat bags dry. Freeze.

TIP *Carrots can be left in the ground, covered with a heavy mulch, and dug up throughout the winter or early in the spring; however, because of melting snows and freezes, I have found this to be an unsatisfactory method of storage in my area of northwestern Vermont.*

Freezing the Standard Way
Good Finished Product

1. Scrub carrots thoroughly; peel. Begin heating water for blanching. Slice or julienne carrots with food processor. Whole carrots do not freeze well.
2. Blanch, 1 pound at a time, by steam or immersion, for 3 to 4 minutes.
3. Cool. Drain well. Pack. Press out air. Seal. Freeze.

Corn

Harvest your corn as soon as the kernels become full and sweet. Corn is at the right stage for picking when you can press milky fluid from the kernels. If the fluid is too clear, the corn is not ready; if it is thick, the corn has gone past its prime and will taste tough and starchy. Starchy corn is best used in cream-style corn.

Some of the newer hybrid, supersweet varieties will retain their prime flavor up to 4 days, if left right on the stalk. Others should be picked as soon as they are ready. Be sure you know which type you planted.

If you must harvest corn before you are ready to process it, harvest it late in the afternoon and do not husk. Place the corn in a large barrel with a layer of ice between each layer of ears. Cover with several layers of newspaper and a lid, if possible. Corn will keep this way for about 24 hours before losing its sweet flavor.

Freezing Unblanched Corn in Husks
Fast and Easy

1. **Harvest** the corn, and do not husk. Place the ears on cookie sheets, or just put them **in the freezer** loose in a single layer. Freeze for 48 hours.
2. **Bag** the corn in a large plastic food-safe bag.
3. Return to freezer. Remove ears as needed. Eat within 4 months.

TIP To cook corn frozen in husks, husk the frozen corn under cold running water. Remove the silks by rotating your hands around the corn. Put the corn in a pan, cover with cool water. Cover the pan, heat to boiling, and boil for 1 minute. Remove from heat, and let the corn stand in hot water for 5 minutes. Eat immediately.

Place corn on cookie sheets.

Freezing Corn on the Cob in Boilable Bags

Fast, Best Finished Product

1. Begin heating water for blanching. Husk cobs, trim, and pack in boilable bags. Add butter if desired. Press out air. Seal.

2. Blanch bags, 4 at time, in boiling water, for 10 minutes. After 5 minutes, turn bags over.

3. Cool in ice water. Pat bags dry. Freeze.

Freeze in single layer.

TIP Corn on the cob frozen in boilable bags should be cooked by placing the bags in cool water. Bring the water to a boil and cook the corn for 10 minutes, turning the package once halfway through the cooking time. Remove from boiling water immediately. Bags of cut corn should be placed in cool water. Bring the water to a boil, and cook for 5 minutes.

Place corn in bag.

Freezing Corn on the Cob the Standard Way

Good Finished Product

1. Husk cobs. Begin heating water for blanching. Trim.
2. Blanch by steam or immersion, 6 ears at a time, for 6 to 8 minutes.
3. Cool. Drain. Pack in bags. Press out air. Seal. Freeze.

Freezing Cream-Style Corn

Excellent Finished Product

1. Husk. Cut corn from cob by cutting down through the center of the kernel. Scrape remaining corn from the cob.
2. Measure kernels as you pour into a large kettle. Add ¼ cup boiling water and 1 teaspoon cornstarch per cup. Stir well. Bring to a boil, simmer for 5 minutes, stirring frequently. Fill sink with ice water while cooking corn.
3. Place kettle in sink of ice water. Stir to cool.
4. Package in rigid containers or bags and freeze.

TIP To cook frozen cream-style corn, place the frozen corn in a double boiler. Add a small amount of milk or light cream, salt, pepper, and a pat of butter. Heat until just piping hot. Let it stand 2 to 3 minutes before serving. To cook in a microwave, place 1 pint frozen corn in a microwave-safe container and cook on HIGH (100% power) for approximately 8 minutes, stirring once halfway through the cooking time.

Whole Kernel Corn in Boilable Bags

Fast Method, Best Finished Product

1. Husk. Begin heating water for blanching. Cut corn from cob. Pack in boilable bags. Add butter if desired. Press out air. Seal bags.
2. Blanch 4 bags at a time in boiling water for 6 minutes.
3. Cool. Pat bags dry. Freeze.

Cucumbers

Cucumbers can be picked at any stage: tiny, for whole pickles; medium, for dill, sliced, or chunk pickles; large, for ripe cucumber pickles. For eating fresh, cucumbers should be harvested when they are 4 to 6 inches long and about 1 to 1½ inches in diameter.

Cucumbers cannot be canned or frozen by any of the regular methods; they must be preserved in brine or vinegar or frozen for salads. Thinly sliced and frozen in brine, they produce a delightfully fresh, crisp flavor to be used in salads all winter.

When cucumbers have reached just the right stage for a specific type of pickle, they should be picked immediately. Even 1 day can allow too much growth. Do not wash cucumbers; store by one of the methods suggested in chapter 2.

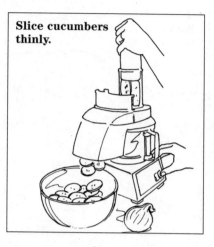

Slice cucumbers thinly.

Freezing Slices for Salads

Fastest Method, Excellent Product

1. Wash 6 to 8 firm, slender cucumbers. Slice thinly with a food processor. Peel and thinly slice 1 medium-size onion. Measure out 2 quarts of sliced cucumbers. Mix with onions and 2 tablespoons of salt in a large bowl.

2. Let stand for 2 hours.

Mix with onions and salt.

SALT

Rinse vegetables.

Add oil, vinegar, and sugar.

SUGAR

VINE

Pack into freezer boxes.

3. Drain vegetables well. Rinse thoroughly with cold water. Drain well again. Return drained vegetables to the rinsed bowl. Add ⅔ cup each of oil, vinegar, and sugar. Add 1 teaspoon celery seed. Mix well.

4. Cover and refrigerate overnight.

5. Pack in freezer jars or rigid freezer containers. Leave 1 inch head space. Freeze.

Note: Can be defrosted and eaten after 1 week. Store defrosted cucumbers in refrigerator. Keep well after defrosting for several weeks.

Eggplant

Ignore the size of the fruit when it comes to harvesting eggplant. Depending on the variety, climate, and soil conditions, your eggplant may vary in size from several inches to a foot or more. The thing to look for is a glossy shine on the skin.

Can't preserve right away? Because eggplant has a fairly neutral flavor and a texture that is so radically altered in cooking, it is perfectly acceptable to store eggplant in a cool place for several days before preserving, provided you harvested when the fruit was firm and glossy, not dull-colored and soft. You will get best results freezing eggplant in your favorite eggplant casserole. Bake the casserole until almost done in a dish lined with aluminum foil, cool and freeze. When frozen solid, remove the dish and leave the casserole wrapped in foil or freezer wrap. When ready to use, unwrap, put back into the original dish, and bake until done. Or freeze in a microwave-safe casserole dish and when ready to use, defrost and heat in the microwave. (For a recipe, see page 172.)

Freezing the Standard Way

Good Finished Product

1. Begin heating 1 gallon water for blanching. Add ¼ cup lemon juice to water to prevent discoloration. Peel the eggplant and cut into slices ½-inch thick.

2. Blanch 1 pound at a time for 4 minutes.

3. Cool in ice water. Drain. Pat dry. Pack. Press out air. Seal. Freeze.

Greens

Spinach to be preserved should be harvested when the leafy portion is 6 inches long. Chard and other greens should be harvested while still young and tender. Chard can be as long as 10 inches. Spinach bolts and turns bitter quickly when the weather warms up, so watch it carefully. Greens should be harvested early in the day while there is still dew on the leaves and before the warming rays of the sun cause them to go limp. If cut at this point they will stay fresh for as long as 2 to 3 days.

Can't preserve right away? Do not wash greens. Store by one of the methods suggested in chapter 2. Avoid placing heavy packages of ice on top of the tender leaves.

Stir-Fry Greens

Fastest Method, Best Finished Product

1. Wash, pick over, drain. Cut through with large knife.

2. Stir-fry until wilted: 2 to 3 minutes.

3. Pack in boilable bags.

4. Cool, pat bags dry, freeze.

TIP Greens can be frozen by using the standard method of freezing. That method takes more time, and since the product is not as good, I do not recommend it.

Chop greens.

Stir-fry until wilted.

Pack into freezer bags.

Transplant lettuce into cold frame.

Lettuce

Late-planted fall lettuce can be harvested right up until the first frost.

Extending the Harvest

1. To preserve lettuce for winter use, plant seed in the garden in late summer.

2. Transplant to a cold frame just before the first frost.

3. Properly cared for, lettuce will continue to produce well into the early winter. See page 201 for a list of reading material on extending the harvest season.

Mushrooms

A bounty of wild mushrooms or a great buy on mushrooms at the store may tempt you to preserve them. Mushrooms can be dried or frozen — just be sure to use commercially grown varieties or those that you know beyond any doubt are nontoxic.

Another simple way to preserve mushrooms is to cook them by sautéing in butter or oil, cooling, then packing in freezer containers.

TIP *To use dried mushooms, place in a bowl, pour in boiling water to cover and let soak for 20 to 30 minutes.*

TIP *To rehydrate dried vegetables quickly, place them in a microwave-safe bowl, cover with cold water, and stir to make sure the vegetables are immersed in the water. Cover and microwave on HIGH (100% power) just to the boiling point. Remove from the oven and let sit until the vegetables are tender.*

Drying Mushrooms

Fastest Method, Excellent Finished Product

1. Wash mushrooms quickly in cold water, without soaking or peeling. Trim ⅛ inch off stem end. Thinly slice or finely chop.

2. Dry in a dehydrator at 120°F for 8 to 12 hours, stirring occasionally and rotating trays once or twice. Well-dried mushrooms should be tough and leathery with no sign of moisture in the center. Or dry in a conventional oven at 120°F for 12 to 18 hours, stirring occasionally and rotating trays once or twice, until leathery and tough. Or dry in the sun for 1 to 2 days until leathery and tough, with no sign of moisture in the centers. Take trays inside at night.

3. Cool and package in airtight containers.

Freezing the Standard Way

Good Finished Product

1. Begin preheating water for blanching. Wash mushrooms quickly in cold water, without soaking or peeling. Trim ⅛ inch off stem end. Leave whole or slice as desired.

2. Blanch, 1 pound at a time, 3 minutes for sliced mushrooms, 5 minutes for whole.

3. Cool mushrooms in ice water. Drain. Pack. Press out air. Seal. Freeze.

Onions, Garlic, and Shallots

Onions, garlic, and shallots, all members of the same family, are the easiest vegetables to harvest and store. Wait until their tops have fallen over in the late summer or early fall and the stems have almost completely dried. Do not try to hasten maturity by bending over the tops before they are ready to fall themselves.

Pull the onions up and allow them to dry in the sun. The longer they are dried before storage, the better they will keep. As a rule of thumb, I never put my onions in storage until the outer skins are totally dry and slip off easily — usually 2 to 3 weeks. I dry my onions on an old screen door that has been placed across sawhorses. This speeds the drying process and prevents rot that could be caused by a week of constant rains.

While cold storage is the easiest and fastest method of storage, having a supply of chopped frozen or dried onions is a great convenience for meal preparation on busy nights.

Pack in mesh bags.

Or braid and hang.

Or chop and freeze in single layer.

One pound of onions can be peeled and chopped in a food processor in 5 minutes. If your supply of stored onions begins to sprout in the spring, tray-freezing or drying the remainder of the crop will prevent a waste of good food.

Cold Storage

Fastest, Easiest Method

The fastest and easiest method of storing dried onions, garlic, and shallots is to pack them into mesh bags and store in a cool, dry area. The next best method is to braid them before the stems are completely dried. Finish drying out in the sun and store in a cool, dry area. It takes me approximately 15 minutes to braid a foot-long string of onions.

TIP *Do not store onions in humid areas. They tolerate cold temperatures as low as 38°F quite well, but will spoil quickly if the humidity is high.*

Tray-Freezing Unblanched Chopped Onions

Convenient End Product

1. Peel and chop or slice onions
2. Spread in a single layer on baking sheets and tray-freeze.
3. Package frozen onions within 12 to 24 hours.

TIP *Freeze a mixture of onions and green or moderately hot peppers to be fried and eaten with hamburgers or frankfurters.*

Drying Chopped Onions
Slowest Method, Convenient End Product

1. Peel and chop onions.
2. Dry in a dehydrator at 120°F for 12 to 24 hours, stirring occasionally and rotating trays once or twice after the first 8 hours, until brittle. Or dry in a conventional oven at 120°F for 24 to 36 hours, stirring occasionally and rotating trays once or twice, until brittle. Or dry in the sun for 2 to 3 days, until brittle and papery.
3. Cool and package in airtight containers.

Peas

Green peas should be harvested as soon as the peas fill the pod. Older peas lose their sweetness quickly and become tough. Harvest from the bottom of the plant first, since these are first to mature. Pick peas late in the afternoon for sweetest flavor. Snow peas must be picked before the pea seed starts to develop. Sugar Snap peas can be picked at any stage, right up until they fill the pod tightly, to freeze for stir-frying, which is the only cooking method I recommend for this variety. If you can't preserve right away, chill your peas immediately by storing according to one of the methods suggested in chapter 2.

TIP *Peas that go past maturity can be left to dry on the vine. Shell and store in dry airtight containers to use in soups.*

Freezing Peas in a Boilable Bag
Fastest, Best Finished Product

1. Begin heating water for blanching; shell peas, wash, and drain. Pack in 1-pint boilable freezer bags. Add butter and seasoning, if desired. Press out air. Seal.
2. Blanch 4 bags at a time in boiling water, for 4 minutes.
3. Cool bags in ice water. Pat dry. Freeze.

Drain peas on towel.

Blanch boilable bag.

Chill in ice water.

TIP *Peas packed in boilable freezer bags can be cooked in the bag in boiling water for 20 minutes. Loosely packed peas are best when steam cooked until barely tender, 5 to 8 minutes.*

Freezing the Standard Way
Excellent Finished Product

1. Shell peas. Preheat water for steam-blanching. Wash peas. Drain.
2. Blanch, 1 pound at a time, for 2 minutes.
3. Cool peas in ice water. Drain. Pack. Press out air. Seal. Freeze.

TIP *Frozen Sugar Snap peas can be chopped and put in tossed salads while still frozen. If they are added just 3 to 4 minutes before the salad is served, they will be crisp, cold, and sweet.*

Blanch and Tray-Freeze Snow and Sugar Snap Peas
Fastest, Best Finished Product

1. Preheat water for steam-blanching. Wash. Trim ends off pods and remove strings.
2. Steam-blanch, 1 pound at a time, for 3 minutes.
3. Cool. Drain.
4. Pat dry. Tray-freeze.
5. When frozen solid, pack in large freezer bags or containers.

TIP *Snow peas and Sugar Snap peas do not retain their crisp texture when frozen; cook by stir-frying.*

Steam-blanch peas.

Chill in ice water.

Drain on towel.

Pat dry.

Freeze in single layer.

Pack into freezer bag.

Remove stem and membrane.

Tray-freeze.

Pack in freezer bags.

Sweet Peppers

For the best frozen or dried product, peppers should be picked when they are fully mature in size and have thick flesh. Since peppers keep well on the bush, there is no need to pick until you are ready to use them. As peppers go past the initial stage of maturity, they will turn red. This does not affect the flavor or texture of the vegetable. I like to freeze some red peppers for added color in soups and casseroles. Peppers can be stored in the refrigerator for up to 2 weeks.

Peppers are a good candidate for drying. While the quickest way to prepare them for drying is to simply cut each in half and deseed, I find it more convenient to use dried diced peppers. Pepper halves must be rehydrated in boiling water for 30 to 45 minutes before using in a recipe, but diced pieces can be added to soups, stews, or rice as it cooks, without any further preparation.

Tray-Freezing Peppers Whole or in Halves

Fastest, Excellent Finished Product

1. Wash; cut out stem end, seed pod, and white membrane.

2. Tray-freeze whole or cut in half.

3. Package frozen peppers in 12 to 24 hours.

Note: Whole or half peppers prepared this way can be stuffed and baked; or sliced, diced, or ground from the frozen state, as needed.

Drying Diced Peppers

Excellent Finished Product

1. Wash; cut out stem end, seed pod, and white membrane. Dice or chop.

2. Dry in a dehydrator at 120°F for 8 to 12 hours, stirring occasionally and rotating trays once or twice. Or dry in a conventional oven at 120°F for 18 to 24 hours, stirring occasionally and rotating trays once, until leathery with no moisture inside. Or dry in the sun for 1 to 2 days, until leathery and completely dry.

3. Cool and package in airtight containers.

Potatoes

Potatoes for winter keeping should not be dug until the tops die off. Once the tops have died, pull the tops from the ground 10 days before digging. This will prevent diseases from starting that could destroy the tubers. Do not wash potatoes before storing. After digging, store at normal temperatures (60 to 75°F) for 10 to 14 days to let the skins dry out enough to prevent moisture loss. The storage area should be protected from light as much as possible; otherwise, potatoes will develop solanine (manifested as a green coloring on the surface), and this can cause illness.

If you do a lot of backpacking, you may want to consider drying some of your potato harvest. Dried potatoes must be watched carefully, however, for any hint of moisture will cause the entire batch to mold. To use, pour 1 cup of boiling water over 1 cup of dried potatoes. Cook 45 to 50 minutes for boiled potatoes or hash browns. One cup dried potatoes yields 1 to 1⅓ cups cooked potatoes.

Cold Storage

Potatoes are easily stored in open boxes, crates, or bins in the warmer area of your root cellar (approximately 40°F) or any cool, dark room or outbuilding. Potatoes stored below 38°F decline in starch and increase in sugar, which destroys their keeping and cooking qualities.

Do not store potatoes in the same root cellar as apples, unless both products are in well-covered containers, and the room is well ventilated.

Store potatoes in crate.

Drying Potatoes
Good Finished Product

1. Wash and peel potatoes. Cut into ½-inch shoestring strips or ⅛–inch slices.

2. Dry in a dehydrator at 120°F for 12 to 18 hours, turning pieces occasionally, until brittle and semi-transparent. Or dry in a conventional oven at 120°F for 18 to 24 hours, turning occasionally and rotating trays once, until brittle. Or dry in the sun for 2 to 3 days, until brittle and semi-transparent. Turn pieces occasionally and take trays inside at night.

3. Cool and package in airtight containers.

Summer Squash

Dried squash is best eaten dried; try it as a snack with a dip, or chop and add directly to salads.

If you can't preserve right away, do not wash the squash. Store by one of the methods suggested in chapter 2.

TIP   *Squash can be sliced ½-inch thick and tray-frozen, unblanched, to be breaded or flour-coated and fried. Do not defrost squash before frying.*

TIP   *Squash to be frozen, dried, or pickled should be harvested when it is small and firm, and the seeds are underdeveloped. Zucchini is at its best when it is 6 to 10 inches long; yellow types, 5 to 7 inches long; and scallop types, about 4 to 5 inches in diameter. Squash grows fast and should not be allowed to remain on the vine past the time it reaches proper size.*

Freezing Unblanched Squash Slices
Fastest, Best Finished Product for Stir-Frying

1. Wash. Drain. Pat dry.
2. Trim ends. Slice no thicker than ¼ inch.
3. Pack in gallon-size freezer bags. Press out air. Seal. Freeze.

Note: Will retain good quality for 4 to 6 months.

TIP Zucchini can be grated and frozen for fruit breads, cookies, and muffins. When defrosting, squeeze the moisture out of squash before measuring and adding to recipe.

TIP For best flavor and texture, cook frozen squash by stir-frying with pork drippings or butter and seasonings (garlic is great), for 2 minutes, or steam for 4 minutes.

TIP Summer squash can be made into pickles and relishes. (See pages 122 and 130 for recipes.)

Freezing Squash in Boilable Bags

Fast, Excellent Finished Product

1. Wash squash. Drain. Pat dry. Trim ends. Slice in ¼-inch slices. Pack in boilable bags. Add butter and seasonings, if desired. Press out air. Seal bags.

2. Blanch bags, 4 at a time, in boiling water for 5 minutes.

3. Cool bags in ice water. Pat bags dry. Freeze.

Drying Squash Chips

Good Finished Product

1. Wash and cut into ⅛-inch slices; do not peel.

Pat squash dry.

Trim ends.

Seal bags.

2. Dry in a dehydrator at 120°F for 6 to 8 hours, turning once, until crisp. Or dry in a conventional oven at 120°F for 6 to 8 hours, until crisp. Or dry in the sun for 8 to 10 hours, turning once, until crisp.

3. Cool and package in airtight containers.

Tomatoes

Pick tomatoes when they are fully ripe and slightly soft to the touch. To be safely canned, tomatoes must be acidified with the addition of citric acid (¼ teaspoon per pint; ½ teaspoon per quart) or lemon juice (1 table-spoon per pint; 2 tablespoons per quart). Although you will find it faster to freeze tomatoes, canning produces a far superior end product.

Drying is a no-fuss way to preserve tomatoes and produces an excellent product, on par with the expensive Italian sun-dried tomatoes.

> *TIP* *At the end of the harvest season, if you would like to hasten the ripening of tomatoes, place them in a single layer in large paper bags, tied loosely. The ethylene gases they release will help them to ripen rapidly and evenly.*

Cold Storage
The Very Fastest Method

Cover with newspaper.

Tomatoes that are good for eating fresh, although not as tasty as summer tomatoes, can be kept fairly well into the early winter if they are properly stored. Pick all large tomatoes just before a hard frost is predicted. Separate the green ones from those more advanced in color. Place the sorted tomatoes in a single layer in shallow boxes or on trays in a root cellar or cool garage. Cover with 2 to 3 layers of newspaper. Check frequently, and remove tomatoes as they ripen. Remove any tomatoes that show signs of spoilage immediately. Green tomatoes stored this way will ripen in 4 to 6 weeks.

> *TIP* *To use whole, unpeeled, frozen tomatoes, run them under tepid water for a few seconds to soften them slightly. Then peel and finish defrosting in a bowl. These tomatoes are best used in sauces, soups, and casseroles.*

TIP *Always defrost tomatoes packaged in plastic bags in a bowl. Use the juice that separates out, as well as the pulp, in order to keep all the nutrients.*

Freezing Whole, Unpeeled Tomatoes
Fastest Method, Less Desirable Product

1. Wash, core tomatoes. Set tomatoes on cookie sheets and freeze.
2. When tomatoes are frozen, pack in bags.

Freezing Whole, Peeled Tomatoes
Good Product, Slow Method

1. Wash tomatoes. Heat water in large kettle to boiling. Refill sink with cold water. Drop tomatoes into boiling water a few at a time. Scald for 30 seconds. Remove to cold water. Lift from water, peel, and core.
2. Pack in rigid containers. Leave 1-inch headspace. Freeze.

Freezing Strained Puree or Juice
Fast Method, Best Freezer Product

1. Wash, core, and quarter tomatoes.
2. Puree through hand-cranked strainer.
3. Pack in rigid containers. Leave 1 inch head space. Freeze.

Note: If you don't have a large hand-cranked strainer, you can make purees and juices with a blender or food mill, but you must cook the tomatoes to soften them before straining.

Puree tomatoes.

Canning Tomato Puree
Best Finished Product

1. Wash, core, and quarter tomatoes.
2. Puree in hand-cranked strainer.
3. Heat puree to boiling. Boil for 5 minutes.

Heat filled canner.

Place lids in water.

Pour puree into jars.

Lower jar into canner.

4. While the puree is heating, preheat the water in the boiling water bath canner and jars. Place the jar lids and screw bands in water according to manufacturer's directions.

5. Pour the hot puree into the heated jars, leaving ½ inch head space. Add citric acid (¼ teaspoon per pint; ½ teaspoon per quart) or lemon juice (1 tablespoon per pint; 2 tablespoons per quart). Add salt (½ teaspoon per pint, 1 teaspoon per quart), if desired.

6. Load canner and process: pints for 35 minutes, quarts for 40 minutes.

TIP   *Freeze or can tomatoes whole or in a puree in the summer; make up sauces, soups, chilis, catsups, relishes, and chutneys, when the woodstove is going in the winter.*

TIP *Tomato juice or puree that is made in a blender or strainer must be heated to boiling and simmered for 5 minutes to remove air; otherwise the jars will not seal properly.*

TIP *To use whole frozen tomatoes in salads, run them under tepid water for a few seconds, peel, and set the tomatoes in a bowl for 30 minutes to soften slightly. Chop and serve in a bowl separate from the salad, to be added to the salad when served. After the tomatoes have been out of the freezer for an hour, they are too soft to use in salads.*

Canning Raw-Packed Whole Tomatoes
Best Finished Product

1. Begin heating water in blancher, boiling water bath canner, and tea kettle. Wash tomatoes. Refill sink or large pan with cold water. Drop tomatoes in boiling water, a few at a time. Scald for 30 seconds. Remove to cold water. Lift tomatoes from cold water. Peel and core tomatoes.

2. Add citric acid (¼ teaspoon per pint; ½ teaspoon per quart) or lemon juice (1 tablespoon per pint; 2 tablespoons per quart) to each hot jar. Pack tomatoes in tightly, leaving ½ inch head space. Add boiling water or juice if necessary to leave ½ inch head space. Add salt (½ teaspoon per pint, 1 teaspoon per quart), if desired.

3. Load canner and process: 40 minutes for pints, 45 minutes for quarts.

Drying Tomato Slices
Fast Method, Excellent Finished Product

1. Wash tomatoes, cut out cores and slice ⅛-inch thick.

2. Dry in a dehydrator at 120°F for 8 to 10 hours, then turn slices and dry for another 6 to 8 hours, until crisp. Or dry in a conventional oven at 120°F for 18 to 24 hours, until crisp, turning slices and and rotating trays once or twice. Or dry in the sun for 1 to 2 days, until brittle, taking the trays in at night.

3. Cool and package in airtight containers.

TIP *For that imported Italian "sun-dried" tomato flavor, pour boiling water over dried tomato slices to partially rehydrate. Drain. Pack in clean jars and cover with extra-virgin olive oil. Add a sprig of basil or a clove of garlic, if desired. Store in a cool place and use within a few months. As long as the tomatoes are completely covered with oil, they will not mold. When the tomatoes are gone, use the oil in cooking and salad dressings; it will have wonderful flavor.*

Winter Squash and Pumpkins

Squash and pumpkins for winter storage should not be picked until they are fully mature and have attained the full color common to their type. Skins should be too hard to be pierced with your thumbnail. Leave at least 1 inch of stem on the fruit when you pick it.

Dry squash in sun.

Wash with bleach and water.

Cool Storage

Fastest, Best Finished Product

1. When harvesting squash and pumpkins, leave them in the sun or warm room (65° to 75°F) for 2 weeks to cure. This will make rinds harder. Acorn squash should be stored without curing.

2. Wash the vegetables with a solution of ½ cup chlorine bleach to a gallon of cold water. This will prevent bacteria growth during storage.

3. Store in a dry, well-ventilated area at 50° to 60°F. Leave space between fruit to allow good air circulation.

Note: Squash and pumpkins should keep well into midwinter when any excess can be frozen or canned.

TIP *For best flavor and texture, reheat frozen squash in boilable bags for 20 minutes or in a double boiler or microwave until piping hot.*

TIP *Steam squash and pumpkins for freezing when the woodstove is going in the winter.*

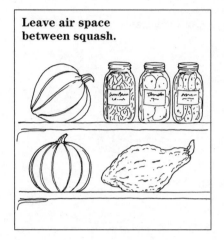

Leave air space between squash.

Freezing Strained Squash in Boilable Bags

Fast Method, Excellent Product

1. Wash squash, cut in quarters or smaller. Steam until tender, 45 to 60 minutes.

2. Scoop out seeds. Scoop out pulp into a hand-cranked strainer and puree (or mash with a potato masher).

3. Pack in 1-pint boilable freezer bags. Add butter and seasoning, if desired. Press out air. Seal bags.

4. Cool. Wipe dry. Freeze.

TIP *Use an ice cream scoop to remove seeds and scoop pulp from rind.*

Mixed Vegetables for Soups and Purees

At the end of the harvest season there is often an abundance of vegetables that have gone past their prime. These vegetables could be composted or fed to the pigs, but freezing vegetables for sauces and soups is an even better way to make use of them.

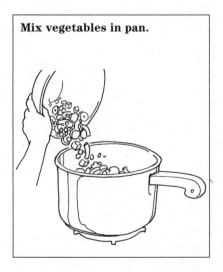

Mix vegetables in pan.

Freezing Mixed Soup Vegetables

Fastest, Best Finished Product

1. Wash 16 to 20 pounds of vegetables. Peel if necessary. Slice, dice, julienne, or chop coarsely.

Chill vegetables in ice water.

Pack in rigid containers.

2. Mix the vegetables in a large pan. Add water to cover. Bring to a boil. Remove from the heat.

3. Cool quickly for 30 minutes.

4. Stir well. Pack in rigid containers. Leave 1-inch headspace. Seal. Freeze.

TIP *To freeze purees, chop the vegetables and cook in a minimum of water until mushy tender. Do not add seasoning. Puree in a hand-cranked strainer, blender, food mill, or fine sieve. Cool quickly and pack in rigid containers; leave 1-inch head space.*

CHAPTER 5

Preserving Each Fruit

MOST OF THE TECHNIQUES THAT APPLY to preserving vegetables apply to preserving fruit. Cold storage works well for apples, grapes, pears, and citrus fruit. Tray-freezing is quick for berries. Apples, cherries, peaches, nectarines, pears, and plums can all be canned. Drying makes sense for fruit, too. Quick snacks of sliced dried fruits or fruit leathers are real kid-pleasers.

As with vegetables, fruits contain enzymes that affect their quality after harvest. With some fruits, natural sugars rapidly convert to starch after harvest; the challenge there is to get the fruit into the freezer or canner or dehydrator as soon as possible. With others, the challenge is to prevent the natural enzymes from causing the fruit to darken and discolor.

Antioxidants Prevent Discoloration

Some fruits, especially apples, peaches, and pears, will discolor if left exposed to the air. The way to avoid this is to work quickly and in small batches, and to treat them with any of the following antioxidants:

1. A commercial preparation such as Fruit-Fresh, according to label directions.

2. One teaspoon or 3,000 mg ascorbic acid (vitamin C) to 1 gallon of water. Dip the fruit in as you go along. Or add ¼ teaspoon ascorbic acid as you pack fruit into jars if you didn't soak them beforehand. Ascorbic acid in crystalline form can be obtained at drugstores.

3. A solution of 2 tablespoons salt and 2 tablespoons vinegar (or 5 tablespoons lemon juice) to 1 gallon cold water. Slice fruit into solution before packing. Work quickly and drain thoroughly; do not leave fruit in water longer than 15 minutes.

> **Please review the basic techniques. Before you start freezing, drying, or canning, turn back to chapter 3 for a quick review of the basic techniques. Assembling all your equipment, setting up a productive work flow, and ensuring the safety of your methods will help to save you time in the long run.**

Sugar Syrups

For canning and freezing most sliced fruits, a sugar syrup is recommended. The sugar is not needed as a preservative, but it does help the fruit maintain a good texture and color. You can substitute honey or maple syrup for the sugar, sweetened or unsweetened fruit juice for the syrup, or plain water. I find that a light sugar syrup makes an excellent product; using unsweetened juices or water leaves the fruit mushy and flat-tasting.

Figure that you will need ½ to ¾ cup syrup or liquid for each pint of fruit; 1 to 1½ cups syrup or liquid for each quart.

Sugar Syrups for Canning and Freezing a 7-Quart Load

	Water or Fruit Juice	Sugar
Very light syrup	10½ cups	1¼ cups
Light syrup	9 cups	2¼ cups
Medium syrup	8¼ cups	3¾ cups
Heavy syrup	7¾ cups	5¼ cups

To make syrups, heat water and sugar together. Bring to a boil and pour over raw fruits in jars for raw packs. For hot packs, bring water and sugar to a boil, add fruit, reheat to boiling, and fill jars immediately.

At the end of each fruit entry, there are instructions for making juice. Since quality fruit juices are readily available in the supermarket, you may not feel the necessity of making juice. However, I've found it worthwhile to make juice from home-grown fruits for making into jelly later in the year, when I am freed from gardening and other preserving tasks, so I include the information here. Juices can be frozen (never skimp on the headspace if you are using glass jars) or canned in a boiling water bath. I can unsweetened juices as most of my juices end up as jelly, where the amount of sugar is specified by the recipe. If you are planning to drink the juice, you can sweeten with a sugar syrup or other sweetener before or after canning or freezing.

It is important to preserve most fruit as soon as possible after harvest. The sugars in ripe fruit begin to convert to starch immediately after harvest. Some fruits, such as pears and apples, are usually picked underripe; these should be put in cold storage as soon as possible, but can be left at room temperature for a day or two if you are planning to preserve them by any other method. Fruits that are to be dried, in particular, should be fully ripe.

Apples

Apples store well in a root cellar and dry beautifully. Applesauce is a staple in most households, and homemade applesauce is far superior to commercial products. Homemade applesauce can be canned or frozen. Finally, apples make great jams and jellies (for recipes, see chapter 8). The natural pectin in apples makes them easy to handle in jams and jellies — they can even be combined with other low-pectin fruits to make a firmer jelly.

Cold Storage
Fastest Method, Best Product

1. Place a large plastic bag in a cardboard box; add 2 to 4 inches of *fresh* sawdust (2 inches for storage areas that will remain above freezing).

2. Add a single layer of apples, leaving a 2-inch space all around the side of the layer to be filled with sawdust. Cover with a 1-inch layer of sawdust. Continue to layer the apples until the box is full. Finish with a 2- to 4-inch layer of sawdust.

3. Fold over the top of the bag and close the box. Store in the coldest area of the root cellar or in an unheated area, such as a garage.

4. Use by the end of the winter.

Drying Apple Slices
Fast Method, Excellent Product

1. Wash and core apples; peeling is optional. Cut in wedges, then in ¼-inch slices; or cut in ¼-inch crosswise rings.

2. Pretreat if drying in the sun. Pretreating is optional with oven-drying and not necessary at all if you work quickly and slice directly onto dehydrator trays. To pretreat, dip slices in ascorbic acid or commerical fruit dip (page 85), then soak for 1 hour in diluted lemon juice (¼ cup lemon juice to 4 cups water) or full-strength pineapple juice.

3. Dry in a dehydrator or in a conventional oven at 115°F for 6 to 8 hours, stirring or turning the fruit once. After the first 6 hours, test for dryness every 2 hours, until there is no moisture in the center when a slice is bitten. Or dry in the sun for 2 to 3 days, until leathery and chewy, with no sign of crispness in the centers. Take trays inside at night.

4. Cool and package in airtight containers.

Freezing Apple Slices with Sugar Syrup

Fast Method, Good Finished Product

1. Prepare medium syrup and set aside. Wash, peel, core, and slice apples. Pretreat with an antioxidant (page 85), if desired.

2. Pack slices in a rigid container and cover with syrup, allowing ½-inch headspace for pints and 1 inch for quarts.

3. Seal and freeze.

Freezing Apple Slices with Sugar

Fast Method, Acceptable Finished Product
for Use in Pies and Baked Goods

1. Wash, peel, core, and slice apples. Pretreat with an antioxidant (page 85), if desired.

2. Sprinkle ¼ cup sugar over each quart of apples; toss to coat well. Allow to stand until juice is drawn out and sugar is dissolved. Pack slices in a rigid container and cover with syrup, allowing ½-inch headspace for pints and 1 inch for quarts.

3. Seal and freeze.

TIP An easy way to freeze apples for pies is to prepare the pie filling as you would if you were baking right away. Freeze slices in a pie tin. When frozen, slip out of the pie tin, wrap in freezer paper, and return to freezer. When you are ready to bake, slip the frozen apples into a prepared pie shell and bake. Thawing first is not necessary.

Freezing Applesauce

Fastest Method for Applesauce, Good Finished Product

1. Wash and quarter apples. Don't peel. Put in heavy-bottomed kettle with 2 inches of water. Cover and cook until soft, stirring occasionally to prevent scorching.

2. Pass through hand-cranked strainer or food mill. Add sweetener to taste, if desired.

3. Cool prepared applesauce and pack into rigid containers leaving ½-inch headspace for pints, 1 inch for quarts.

TIP *Thawing applesauce takes some time, unless you have a microwave oven. You may find it more convenient to can the applesauce than to freeze it.*

Making Apple Fruit Leather

Excellent Finished Product

1. Core and cut up 4 medium-size apples, without peeling. Add ½ cup water and cook over medium heat for 15 to 20 minutes, or until tender. Force through a sieve or colander and stir in ¼ cup honey.

2. Line a drying tray with plastic wrap (or use the fruit leather sheet that came with your dehydrator). Spread the puree ⅛-inch thick on the trays.

3. Dry in a dehydrator at 120°F for 6 to 8 hours, or until leather can be pulled easily from plastic. Invert, pull off plastic, and continue drying for another 4 to 6 hours. Dry in the oven at 120°F for 6 to 8 hours or until leather can be pulled easily from plastic. Invert, pull off plastic, and continue drying for another 6 to 8 hours. Dry in the sun for 1 day, or until leather can be pulled easily from plastic. Invert, pull off plastic, and dry for 1 more day.

4. To store, roll up in waxed paper or plastic wrap, close and twist ends, and store in the refrigerator for up to 6 weeks.

Canning Applesauce

Slow Method, Excellent Finished Product

Even though it takes time to make applesauce, it yields such a wonderful finished product that you may find it well worth your time. Figure that 21 pounds of apples will yield a canner load of 7 quarts of applesauce.

1. Wash and quarter apples. Don't peel. Put in heavy-bottomed kettle with 2 inches of water. Cover and cook until soft, stirring occasionally to prevent scorching. Begin preheating water in canner and tea kettle and preparing jars and lids.

2. Pass softened apples through a hand-cranked strainer or food mill. Add sweetener to taste, if desired. Reheat sauce to boiling.

3. Pack hot applesauce in hot clean jars, leaving ½-inch headspace. Process pints for 15 minutes, quarts for 20 minutes.

Making Apple Juice (Frozen or Canned)
Good Finished Product

1. Sterilize jars for canning or prepare containers for freezing. Begin heating water in canner, if using.

2. Select a variety of apples for best flavor. Wash and quarter; do not peel or core. Place in a saucepan and cover with boiling water. Heat and simmer until soft, 25 to 30 minutes.

3. Press through a damp jelly bag or double layers of cheesecloth. Strain again through cheesecloth or coffee filter paper.

4. To freeze, pour into freezer containers, leaving 1½-inch headspace. Freeze.

5. To can, reheat juice, stirring occasionally, to boiling. Pour into hot jars, leaving ¼-inch head space. Process pints or quarts for 5 minutes.

Apricots

Dried apricots are a real treat, and with apricot season so brief, it may be that more apricots are consumed dried than fresh or canned. Select perfectly ripe apricots for preserving. The fruit should not be mushy, but green fruit does not dry well and will not have full flavor after it is canned or frozen.

Drying Apricot Halves
Fast Method, Excellent Product

1. Peel apricots by dipping in boiling water for 1 minute, then in ice water for 1 minute. Skins will slip off easily. Cut in half, removing the seeds.

2. Dip in commercial fruit dip or ascorbic acid solution (see page 85).

3. Dry in a dehydrator at 115°F for 36 to 48 hours, stirring or turning the fruit occasionally and rotating trays, until the fruit is leathery. Dry in a conventional oven at 115°F for 2 to 3 days, stirring or turning the fruit occasionally and rotating trays, until the fruit is leathery. Or dry in the sun for 4 or more days, until leathery. Take trays inside at night.

4. Cool and package in airtight containers.

TIP *To speed drying, spread halves, pit side up, on trays and dry until they begin to wrinkle. Turn halves over and flatten with the hand, a spatula, or a block of wood.*

Freezing Apricot Halves with Sugar Syrup

Fast Method, Good Finished Product

1. Prepare medium syrup (page 86). Add ¾ teaspoon of crystalline ascorbic acid to each quart of syrup, and set aside. Dip apricots in boiling water for 1 minute, then in ice water for 1 minute. Peel, cut in half, and remove pits.

2. Pack in a rigid container and cover with syrup, allowing ½-inch headspace for pints and 1 inch for quarts.

3. Seal and freeze.

Freezing Apricot Halves with Sugar

Fast Method, Acceptable Finished Product

1. Dip apricots in boiling water for 1 minute, then in ice water for 1 minute. Peel, cut in half, and remove pits.

2. Sprinkle ¼ teaspoon ascorbic acid dissolved in ¼ cup water over each quart of apricots. Mix ½ cup of sugar with each quart of apricots, toss to coat well. Allow to stand until juice is drawn out and sugar is dissolved.

3. Pack slices in a rigid container, allowing ½-inch headspace for pints and quarts.

4. Seal and freeze.

Making Apricot Fruit Leather

1. Dip ripe apricots in boiling water for 1 minute, then in ice water. Slip off skins and cut in half. Remove pits and process in a blender until pureed.

2. Line a drying tray with plastic wrap (or use the fruit leather sheet that came with your dehydrator). Spread the puree ⅛-inch thick on the trays.

3. Dry in a dehydrator at 120°F for 6 to 8 hours, or until leather can be pulled easily from plastic. Invert, pull off plastic, and continue drying for another 4 to 6 hours. Dry in a conventional oven at 120°F for 6 to 8 hours or until leather can be pulled easily from plastic. Invert, pull off plastic, and continue drying for another 6 to 8 hours. Dry in the sun for 1 day, or until leather can be pulled easily from plastic. Invert, pull off plastic, and dry for 1 more day.

4. To store, roll up in waxed paper or plastic wrap, close and twist ends, and store in the refrigerator for up to 6 weeks.

Raw-Pack Canning Apricot Halves
Slowest Method, Excellent Finished Product

Figure that 16 pounds of fruit will yield 7 quarts. Select firm apricots that are ready for eating.

1. Dip in boiling water for 1 minute, then in ice water. Slip off skins, cut in half, and remove pits. Place in ascorbic acid solution (see page 85). Prepare very light, light, or medium syrup (page 86), if using.
2. Begin preheating water in canner and tea kettle. Prepare jars and lids for hot pack. Heat syrup or juice.
3. Drain fruit and pack into hot jars, leaving ½-inch headspace. Pack fruit cut-side down. Fill with hot liquid, leaving ½-inch headspace.
4. Process pints for 25 minutes, quarts for 30 minutes.

Blueberries

Tray-Freezing Whole Berries
Fastest Method, Excellent Finished Product

1. Wash berries and drain on absorbent toweling. Pat dry with another towel.
2. Place dry berries on wax-paper-lined cookie sheets and freeze until solid.
3. Within 24 hours, package loosely in plastic bags and return to freezer.

Freezing Blueberries in Sugar
Fast Method, Excellent Finished Product

1. Wash berries and drain on absorbent toweling. Pat dry with another towel.
2. Add ½ cup of sugar to each quart of berries and mix well.
3. Pack into containers, leaving ½-inch headspace.
4. Seal and freeze.

TIP   *Berries packed with sugar retain their texture better than berries frozen unsweetened. The best way to preserve berries for use in pies is with sugar.*

Drying Whole Berries

Fast Method, Good Finished Product

1. Dip in boiling water for 30 seconds to split the skins.
2. Dry the berries in a dehydrator at 115°F for 12 to 24 hours, stirring occasionally and rotating trays, until the fruit is hard but still chewy. Dry in an oven at 115°F for 18 to 36 hours, stirring occasionally and rotating trays, until the fruit is hard but still chewy. Or dry in the sun for 2 to 4 days, until hard but chewy. Take trays inside at night.
3. Cool and package in airtight containers.

TIP *For extra flavor, blueberries can be dipped in a honey solution before drying. Dissolve 1 cup of sugar in 3 cups hot water. Cool to lukewarm and stir in 1 cup honey. Dip berries in solution and remove with a slotted spoon. Drain well before drying.*

TIP *Honey-dipped or plain, dried berries and cherries are delicious eaten as a confection. They can be directly added to breakfast cereals and muffin and cake batters.*

Cherries

Freezing Tart Cherries in Sugar

Fast Method, Excellent Finished Product

1. Wash cherries, stem, and pit, using a cherry pitter or sharp paring knife.
2. Add ¾ cup of sugar to each quart of cherries and mix well.
3. Pack into containers, leaving ½-inch headspace.
4. Seal and freeze.

Freezing Sweet Cherries in Sugar Syrup

Fast Method, Good Finished Product

1. Prepare heavy syrup (page 86) and set aside. Wash and pit cherries.
2. Pack cherries in a rigid container and cover with syrup, allowing ½-inch headspace for pints and 1 inch for quarts.
3. Seal and freeze.

Drying Whole Cherries

Fastest Method, Good Finished Product

1. Wash and pit fully ripe sweet or tart cherries. Drain well.
2. Dry untreated cherries in a dehydrator at 115°F for 24 hours, stirring occasionally and rotating trays, until the fruit is chewy but dry. Dry in a conventional oven at 115°F for 18 to 36 hours, stirring occasionally and rotating trays, until the cherries are dry but still chewy. Or dry in the sun for 4 to 5 days, until chewy but dry. Take trays inside at night.
3. Cool and package in airtight containers.

TIP   *Dried sweet or tart cherries are a delicious alternatives to raisins and can be used in exactly the same ways.*

Making Cherry Fruit Leather

1. Pit 2 cups tart cherries. Combine in a blender with ½ cup sugar. Process until sugar is dissolved and fruit is pureed.
2. Line a drying tray with plastic wrap (or use the fruit leather sheet that came with your dehydrator). Spread the puree ⅛-inch thick on the trays.
3. Dry in a dehydrator at 120°F for 6 to 8 hours, or until leather can be pulled easily from plastic. Invert, pull off plastic, and continue drying for another 4 to 6 hours. Dry in a conventional oven at 120°F for 6 to 8 hours or until leather can be pulled easily from plastic. Invert, pull off plastic, and continue drying for another 6 to 8 hours. Dry in the sun for 1 day, or until leather can be pulled easily from plastic. Invert, pull off plastic, and dry for 1 more day.
4. To store, roll up in waxed paper or plastic wrap, close and twist ends, and store in the refrigerator for up to 6 weeks.

Raw-Pack Canning Sweet or Sour Cherries

Slowest Method, Excellent Finished Product

Figure that 17½ pounds of fruit will yield 7 quarts. Select bright, uniformly colored cherries.

1. Stem and wash cherries. Pit with cherry pitter or paring knife.
2. Begin preheating water in canner and tea kettle. Prepare jars and lids according to the manufacturer's recommendations.
3. Prepare syrup of any weight (page 86), if using, and keep warm. Or heat to boiling water, apple juice, or white grape juice and keep warm.
4. Add ½ cup hot syrup, juice, or water to each jar. Fill with cherries,

shaking down gently as you fill. Add more hot liquid, leaving ½-inch headspace.

5. Process pints or quarts for 25 minutes.

Cranberries

Although cranberries are not a gardener's delight, they are a wonderful fruit that is available in the supermarkets for only a few short months each year. Freezing is by far the easiest method of preserving these under-utilized berries, but drying is a good alternative, if only because dried cranberries make such a delightful alternative to raisins in baked goods.

Freezing Whole Cranberries
Fastest Method, Best Finished Product

Simply place the cranberries, still in their original packaging, in the freezer. No washing or processing is necessary.

Drying Whole Cranberries
Fast Method, Good Finished Product

1. Dip in boiling water for 30 seconds to split skins. Drain well.

2. Dry untreated berries in a dehydrator at 115°F for 12 to 24 hours, stirring occasionally and rotating trays, until the fruit is hard but still chewy. Dry in a conventional oven at 115°F for 18 to 36 hours, stirring occasionally and rotating trays, until fruit is hard but still chewy. Or dry in the sun for 2 to 4 days, until hard but chewy. Take trays inside at night.

3. Cool and package in airtight containers.

TIP *For extra flavor, cranberries can be dipped in a honey solution before drying. Dissolve 1 cup of sugar in 3 cups hot water. Cool to lukewarm and stir in 1 cup honey. Dip berries in solution and remove with a slotted spoon. Drain well before drying.*

Canning Cranberry Sauce
Slowest Method, Excellent Finished Product

1. Begin preheating water in canner and tea kettle. Prepare jars and lids.

2. Combine 8 cups fresh or frozen cranberries with 2 cups water in a saucepan. Cook until berries are soft. Add 4 cups sugar and boil for 3 minutes.

3. Pack into hot jars, leaving ½-inch headspace.

4. Process pints and quarts for 15 minutes.

Grapes

Cold Storage

Fastest Method, Best Finished Product

1. Place a large plastic bag in a cardboard box; add 2 to 4 inches of *fresh* sawdust (2 inches for storage areas that will remain above freezing).

2. Add a single layer of grapes, leaving a 2-inch space all around the side of the layer to be filled with sawdust. Cover with a 1-inch layer of sawdust. Continue to layer the grapes until the box is full. Finish with a 2- to 4-inch layer of sawdust.

3. Fold over the top of the bag and close the box. Store in the coldest area of the root cellar or in an unheated area, such as a garage.

4. Use within 1 to 2 months.

Raisins

Fast Method, Good Finished Product

1. Leave whole, or cut in half. Seed as needed. Whole seedless grapes should be dipped in boiling water for 30 seconds to split skins. Drain well.

2. Dry grapes in a dehydrator at 115°F for 24 to 48 hours, stirring occasionally and rotating trays, until the fruit is dry to the center. Dry in a conventional oven at 115°F for 48 to 72 hours, stirring occasionally and rotating trays, until wrinkled and dry to the center. Or dry in the sun for 3 to 5 days, until wrinkled and dry to the center. Take trays inside at night.

3. Cool and package in airtight containers.

Making Grape Juice

Slowest Method, Excellent Finished Product

1. Wash and stem grapes. Place in a saucepan and cover with boiling water. Heat and simmer until skins are soft. Strain through a damp jelly bag or double layers of cheesecloth. Refrigerate juice for 24 to 48 hours. Without mixing the juice, carefully pour off the clear liquid, and discard any sediment in the bottom of the container.

2. Begin heating water in tea kettle and canner, if using. Sterilize jars for canning or prepare containers for freezing.

3. To freeze, pour into freezer containers, leaving 1½ inches headspace.

4. To can, pour into sterilized, hot jars, leaving ¼-inch headspace. Process pints or quarts for 5 minutes.

Nectarines and Peaches

Freezing Nectarines and Peaches in Sugar

Fast Method, Excellent Finished Product

1. Peel ripe peaches by briefly dipping into boiling water, then in ice water. Slip off the skins, cut in half, and remove pits. Nectarines do not need peeling.

2. Add ⅔ cup of sugar to each quart of fruit and mix well.

3. Pack into containers, leaving 1-inch headspace.

4. Seal and freeze.

Freezing Nectarines and Peaches in Sugar Syrup

Fast Method, Excellent Finished Product

1. Prepare medium syrup (page 86) and set aside. To peel, briefly dip peaches in boiling water, then in ice water. Slip off skins, slice in half, and remove pit. Nectarines do not require peeling.

2. Pack in a rigid container and cover with syrup, allowing ½-inch headspace for pints and 1 inch for quarts.

3. Seal and freeze.

Drying Nectarine and Peach Halves

Fast Method, Good Product

1. Peel peaches by dipping in boiling water for 1 minute, then in cold water for 1 minute. Skins will slip off easily. Cut in half, removing the seeds. Nectarines do not need peeling.

2. Dip in commercial fruit dip or ascorbic acid solution (page 85).

3. Dry in a dehydrator at 115°F for 24 to 36 hours, stirring or turning the fruit occasionally and rotating trays, until the fruit is leathery with no hint of moisture when bitten. Dry in a conventional oven at 115°F for 36 to 48 hours, stirring or turning the fruit occasionally and rotating trays, until the fruit is leathery with no hint of moisture when bitten. Or dry in the sun for 4 to 6 days, until leathery and almost stiff, with no hint of moisture in the center. Take trays inside at night.

4. Cool and package in airtight containers.

TIP To speed drying, spread halves, pit side up, on trays and dry until they begin to wrinkle. Turn halves over and flatten with the hand, a spatula, or a block of wood.

Making Nectarine and Peach Fruit Leather

1. Select ripe or slightly overripe fruit. Peel and cut in halves. Remove pits and puree in blender.

2. Line a drying tray with plastic wrap (or use the fruit leather sheet that came with your dehydrator). Spread the puree ⅛-inch thick on the trays.

3. Dry in a dehydrator at 120°F for 6 to 8 hours, or until leather can be pulled easily from plastic. Invert, pull off plastic, and continue drying for another 4 to 6 hours. Dry in a conventional oven at 120°F for 6 to 8 hours or until leather can be pulled easily from plastic. Invert, pull off plastic, and continue drying for another 6 to 8 hours. Dry in the sun for 1 day, or until leather can be pulled easily from plastic. Invert, pull off plastic, and dry for 1 more day.

4. To store, roll up in waxed paper or plastic wrap, close and twist ends, and store in the refrigerator for up to 6 weeks.

Canning Nectarine and Peach Halves
Slowest Method, Excellent Finished Product

Figure that 17½ pounds of fruit will yield 7 quarts. Select ripe mature fruit that is ready for eating.

1. Briefly dip peaches in boiling water, then in ice water. Slip off skins, cut in half, and remove pits. Nectarines do not need peeling. Place in ascorbic acid solution (see page 85). Prepare very light, light, or medium syrup (page 86), if using.

2. Begin preheating water in canner and tea kettle. Prepare jars and lids.

3. Drain fruit and pack cut side down in jars, leaving ½-inch headspace.

4. Fill jars with hot syrup, water, or fruit juice, leaving ½-inch headspace.

5. Process pints for 25 minutes, quarts for 30.

Pears

Cold Storage
Fastest Method, Best Finished Product

1. Place a large plastic bag in a cardboard box; add 2 to 4 inches of *fresh* sawdust (2 inches for storage areas that will remain above freezing).

2. Add a single layer of slightly immature pears, leaving a 2-inch space all around the side of the layer to be filled with sawdust. Cover with a 1-inch layer of sawdust. Continue to layer the pears until the box is full. Finish with a 2- to 4-inch layer of sawdust.

3. Fold over the top of the bag and close the box. Store in the coldest area of the root cellar or in an unheated area, such as a garage.

4. Use by the end of winter.

Freezing Pears in Sugar Syrup

Good Finished Product

1. Prepare a syrup by mixing in a ratio of 3 cups sugar to 4 cups water. Bring to a boil, then let cool.

2. Wash, peel, and core pears. Place in an antioxidant (page 85).

3. Drain pears and blanch for 2 minutes in boiling water to cover. Cool in ice water immediately. Drain. Pack in a rigid container and cover with syrup, allowing ½-inch headspace for pints and 1 inch for quarts.

4. Seal and freeze.

Hot Pack Canning Pear Halves

Slowest Method, Excellent Finished Product

Figure that 16 pounds of fruit will yield 7 quarts. Select firm pears that are ready for eating.

1. Begin preheating water in canner and tea kettle. Prepare jars and lids.

2. Wash and peel pears. Cut in half and core pears (a melon baller works well). Place in ascorbic acid solution (see page 85). Prepare very light, light, or medium syrup (page 86), if using.

3. Drain pears and combine in a large saucepan with syrup or water, apple juice, or white grape juice. Bring to a boil and boil for 5 minutes.

4. Fill hot jars with hot fruit, cut–side down, and cooking liquid, leaving ½-inch headspace. Place halves in layers.

5. Process pints for 20 minutes, quarts for 25 minutes.

Pineapples

Freezing Unsweetened Pineapple Slices

Fastest Method, Good Finished Product

1. Wash, slice, and pare pineapple. Pack into containers, leaving ½-inch headspace.

2. Seal and freeze.

Freezing Pineapple Slices in Sugar Syrup

Fast Method, Excellent Finished Product

1. Prepare thin syrup (page 86) made with water or pineapple juice and set aside. Wash, slice, and pare pineapple.
2. Pack slices in a rigid container and cover with syrup, allowing ½-inch headspace for pints and 1 inch for quarts.
3. Seal and freeze.

Drying Pineapple Slices

Fast Method, Good Product

1. Cut pineapple into 1-inch slices. Peel and core each slice. No pretreatment is necessary, but dipping in a honey solution as with blueberries (see page 93) is highly recommended.
2. Dry in a dehydrator at 115°F for 24 to 36 hours, stirring or turning the fruit occasionally and rotating trays, until the fruit is chewy and dried through. Dry in a conventional oven at 115°F for 36 to 48 hours, stirring or turning the fruit occasionally and rotating trays, until the fruit is chewy and dried through. Or dry in the sun for 4 to 5 days, until the fruit is chewy and dried through. Take trays inside at night.
3. Cool and package in airtight containers.

Hot-Pack Canning Pineapple Slices

Slowest Method, Excellent Finished Product

1. Begin preheating water in canner and tea kettle. Prepare jars and lids for hot pack.
2. Peel and remove eyes and tough fibers from pineapple. Slice.
3. Prepare very light, light, or medium syrup (page 86), if using.
4. Combine pineapple in a large saucepan with syrup, water or pineapple juice. Bring to a boil and simmer for 10 minutes.
5. Fill jars with hot fruit and cooking liquid, leaving ½-inch headspace.
6. Process pints for 15 minutes, quarts for 20 minutes.

Plums

Drying Whole Prunes

Fastest Method, Excellent Finished Product

1. Wash and dip in boiling water for 1 minute to crack skins.
2. Dry in a dehydrator at 115°F for 18 to 24 hours, turning the fruit and

rotating the trays every few hours, until the fruit is chewy but dry in the center. Dry in a conventional oven at 115°F for 24 to 36 hours, stirring or turning the fruit occasionally and rotating trays, until the fruit is chewy but dry in the center. Or dry in the sun for 36 to 48 hours, until the fruit is chewy but dry in the center. Take trays inside at night.

3. Cool and package in airtight containers.

Raw-Pack Canning Plums
Slowest Method, Good Finished Product

1. Begin preheating water in canner and tea kettle. Prepare jars and lids.
2. Prick skins on 2 sides of plums to prevent splitting. Freestone plums can be halved and pitted, if desired. Prepare very light, light, or medium syrup (page 86), if using.
3. Fill jars with fruit and hot water, syrup or juice, leaving ½-inch headspace.
4. Process pints for 20 minutes, quarts for 25 minutes.

Raspberries

Tray-Freezing Whole Berries
Fastest Method, Excellent Finished Product

1. Wash berries and drain on absorbent toweling. Pat dry with another towel.
2. Place dry berries on wax-paper-lined cookie sheets and freeze until solid.
3. Within 24 hours, package loosely in plastic bags and return to freezer.

Freezing Berries in Sugar
Fast Method, Excellent Finished Product

1. Wash berries and drain on absorbent toweling. Pat dry with another towel.
2. Add ½ cup of sugar to each quart of berries and mix well.
3. Pack into containers, leaving ½-inch headspace.
4. Seal and freeze.

TIP Berries packed with sugar retain their texture better than berries frozen unsweetened. The best way to preserve berries for use in pies is with sugar.

Rhubarb

As soon as the stalks are as thick as your thumb, it is time to harvest rhubarb. Since there are both green and red varieties, don't use color as an indicator of readiness. To harvest, twist (don't cut) the outside stalks. Be sure to cut out the seed pods as they form in the center of the plant to prolong the harvest.

Since rhubarb is always eaten stewed or baked in a pie or cooked in a jam — preferably with plenty of sweetener — we are less concerned with texture here than we are with most fruits. Frozen rhubarb can be defrosted and made into jam at a later date.

Freezing Unsweetened Rhubarb

Fastest, Easiest, Excellent Finished Product

1. Wash and trim off both ends of each stalk. Cut into 1-inch pieces. (The leaves contain oxalic acid, which is poisonous, so dispose of them where the children will not find them.)
2. Pack into containers, leaving ½-inch headspace. Seal and freeze.

Canning Sweetened Rhubarb

Time-Consuming Method, Excellent Finished Product

1. Wash and trim off both ends of each stalk. Cut into 1-inch pieces. (The leaves contain oxalic acid, which is poisonous, so dispose of them where the children will not find them.)
2. Add ½ cup sugar to each quart of sliced fruit. Let stand for several hours to draw out the juice.
3. Begin heating water in canner and tea kettle. Prepare jars and lids.
4. Boil the rhubarb for 1 minute.
5. Pack into clean hot jars, leaving ½-inch headspace. Cover with hot juice, leaving ½-inch headspace. Process pints and quarts for 10 minutes.

Strawberries

Tray-Freezing Whole Berries

Fastest Method, Good Finished Product

1. Wash berries and drain on absorbent toweling. Hull. Pat dry with another towel.
2. Place dry berries on wax-paper-lined cookie sheets and freeze until solid.

3. Within 24 hours, package loosely in plastic bags and return to freezer.

Freezing Berries in Sugar

Fast Method, Excellent Finished Product

1. Wash berries and drain on absorbent toweling. Hull. Pat dry with another towel.
2. Add ¾ cup of sugar to each quart of berries and mix well.
3. Pack into containers, leaving ½-inch headspace.
4. Seal and freeze.

TIP *Berries packed with sugar retain their texture better than berries frozen unsweetened. Sweetened frozen strawberries can be thawed and served as a topping for pancakes, shortcake, or ice cream. Tray-frozen berries are best served semi-thawed so as to retain their shape.*

TIP *Frozen fruit can be easily defrosted in a microwave. Set the microwave on DEFROST (30% power) and defrost 1-pint containers for 5 to 6 minutes and 1-quart containers for 9 to 10 minutes.*

CHAPTER 6

Preserving Herbs

THE MOST COMMON WAY to preserve herbs is to dry them. However, many herbs can be frozen, with the end product closer to fresh than dried. Frozen herbs, however, appear limp and are sometimes discolored, so they will not be suitable to use as garnishes or with most raw foods. However, frozen herbs are excellent in cooked dishes.

Herbs can be preserved in pestos or other herb pastes, which freeze beautifully. Also, herbs can be preserved in teas, vinegars, and jellies. In this chapter, I start with drying herbs and freezing herbs, and then give methods and recipes for various herbal products.

Drying Herbs: Fast and Convenient

Pick leaves and flowers for drying when the flower buds are about half open. If seeds are being harvested, they should be collected when the seed heads are turning brown. Pick before noon, as soon as the sun has dried off the dew. Use pruning shears to harvest, leaving about 4 inches of stem on annual herbs and about two thirds of the stem on perennial herbs to permit further growth.

Wash herbs under running water or spray. Shake to remove moisture and pat dry. Inspect leaves for dirt and insects as you move through the process.

The flavor of most dried herbs is much more pronounced than fresh herbs, so it is important to use very small amounts in cooking. A few herbs, including parsley, cilantro, and chives, lose flavor when dried and are far superior fresh or frozen.

Hang-Drying Herbs
Fastest, Easiest Method

Hang-drying is definitely the fastest, easiest, and most popular way to preserve herbs. Just tie the freshly picked herbs in small bunches and hang them upside down in a warm, dark, airy place. Some people place the herb bundles in paper bags with air holes punched in them to reduce the exposure to light and dust, but this isn't necessary if you are drying in a dark, airy attic.

The herbs should be dry in about 2 weeks — or when they crumble to the touch. Don't forget about them; allowing them to hang for too long reduces their quality.

Strip the leaves, crumble, and store in small glass jars. Keep in a cool, dry, dark place.

TIP *If your microwave oven manufacturer doesn't warn against using a microwave for herb drying, you can give it a try. Place a single layer of herb leaves between paper towels and dry for 1 to 2 minutes, depending on the thickness of the leaves. Remove paper towels. When dry, herbs will crumble in the hands. If not dry, return leaves to the microwave and dry at 1-minute intervals. Do not overdry; herbs will taste charred and may even catch fire.*

Dehydrator Drying

Be sure to dry only one type of herb at a time. Arrange herbs in a thin layer on dehydrator trays. Dry according to the times listed for each individual herb on pages 111–113, from 4 to 18 hours depending on the fleshiness of the leaves. Crumble and store in small glass jars. Keep in a cool, dry, dark place.

Oven-Drying Herbs
Easy and Quick

To keep flavors from mingling, dry only one type of herb at a time. Heat your oven to 200°F. Turn off the heat. Place a rack of herb leaves in the oven and leave for 6 to 8 hours or overnight. Or dry according to the direction given for each individual herb on pages 111–113.

Crumble and store in small glass jars. Keep in a cool, dry, dark place.

Freezing Herbs

Some of the thick, leafy herbs, such as parsley and basil, can be frozen. Frozen herbs have the same pungency as fresh herbs, though they lack the crisp, fresh texture. Some herbs, like chives and cilantro, are better frozen than dried.

Freezing Herbs in Bags

Fastest, Easiest Method

To freeze herbs, gently wash freshly picked herbs, if necessary. Blot dry. Strip the leaves off the stalks and chop or leave whole. Pack into bags or containers, seal, and freeze.

Freezing Herb Pastes

A convenient way to preserve herbs is chopped and blended with enough oil to make a paste. This paste can be stored in the refrigerator for up to a month or frozen for up to 6 months. Herb pastes can be made into pesto — the traditional Italian herb paste made with basil, olive oil, parmesan cheese, and pine nuts — to dress pasta or add flavor to soups, stews, or salad dressings. A recipe for Pesto Pasta is found on page 180.

1. Coarsely chop 2 cups fresh herb leaves in a food processor.
2. Slowly drizzle in ⅓ cup high-quality olive or other salad oil while the motor is still running.
3. For immediate use, pack the herbs in small jars; remove any air bubbles by running a knife through the mixture. Cover the top of the mixture with more oil to seal out any air, and refrigerate. For long-term storage, pack in jars, seal with oil, and freeze.

To have small quantities readily available for adding to a dish, line a baking sheet with waxed paper, drop the mixture by the tablespoon onto the cookie sheet. Cover with plastic wrap and freeze. When frozen solid, place frozen mounds of herb paste in a plastic bag, seal, and return to freezer.

TIP *Basil is traditionally transformed into a delicious herb paste known as pesto. Other herbs that will make delicious herb pastes include chervil, cilantro, dill, fennel, marjoram, mint, parsley, rosemary, sage, savory, and tarragon.*

Freezing Herbs in Ice Cubes
Convenient for Soups and Stews

Wash and dry the herbs. Chop and spoon into an ice cube tray. Pour water over them and freeze. Pop them out of the tray and into the cooking pot as needed.

Herbal Products

The harvest season for herbs extends throughout the summer. Somehow it always seems like there's enough time to make teas and vinegars, perhaps because they are usually made in small quantities. Also, you can make teas and vinegars with dried herbs, so even if the harvest season finds you flat out with gardening and preserving chores, you will probably be able to find some time during the year for making herb teas, vinegars, and jellies.

Herb Teas

Herb teas made from the dried leaves of herbs can be soothing or invigorating, spicy or mellow; good for serving hot or cold. It all depends on which herbs you select. There are no rules for combining herbs. You will have to experiment until you find a mix you like best.

Herb teas are usually steeped in hot water, but not boiled. Simply place 1 teaspoon of dried herb (or 1 tablespoon fresh herbs) into a tea strainer. Put this in a tea cup and pour boiling water over it. Allow to steep for 5 to 7 minutes. Sweeten with honey or sugar, if desired.

> *Favorite Herbs for Tea*
>
> *Camomile*
> *Lemon balm*
> *Lemongrass*
> *Lemon verbena*
> *Mint*
> *Rose hips*

Herb Vinegars

Herb-flavored vinegars add zing to a salad and provide a wonderful way to preserve the sprightly flavor of fresh herbs. Plus, they are very easy to make.

Select any herb, or combination of herbs, that you like. Wine vinegar is recommended as a base, as cider and white vinegars are so strongly flavored, they easily overpower the delicate herb flavor. As a general rule, white wine vinegar is used when color is important, such as with chive blossoms or opal basil, and red wine vinegar is used for strong flavors, such as basil, oregano, and garlic.

To make herb vinegar, follow these steps:

1. Place 1 cup of washed and dried fresh herbs in a sterilized quart jar. Pour 3 to 3½ cups vinegar over the herbs.

2. Seal the jar and place in a cool, dark spot for 4 to 6 weeks, shaking the mixture every few days. Taste. If the mixture is too herbal, dilute with more vinegar. If the mixture isn't flavorful enough, repeat the procedure with fresh herbs.

3. Strain through a plastic (not metal) colander to remove the herbs. Then strain through paper coffee filters until the vinegar is crystal clear.

4. Pour the vinegar into hot, sterilized, dry jars. Add a sprig or two of fresh, washed, and dried herbs. Fill with strained vinegar and cap immediately.

TIP *Marjoram, opal basil, burnet, chive blossom, tarragon, thyme, nasturtium, rosemary, lavender, and rose petals are best with white wine vinegars. For red wine vinegar, choose strongly flavored herbs, such as basil, dill, garlic, sage, fennel, lovage, spearmint or peppermint, bay, thyme, chive, caraway, or savory.*

Herb Jellies

Herb jellies provide yet another way to preserve herbs. Mint jelly is a traditional accompaniment to lamb, but the possible combinations are infinite. Thyme jellies are delicious with beef or fish; sage jelly goes well with poultry; basil jelly goes well with just about any meal.

If you are making apple jelly anyway, consider adding a few herb leaves to each hot, sterilized jar for an exciting new flavor. Otherwise, you will need to start with an herb infusion — herbs that have been steeped in a hot liquid for about 20 minutes. You may use homemade or commercial fruit juice or water as the base.

Please review the instructions for making jams and jellies in chapter 8 before proceeding with the recipe.

⁓ *Basic Herb Jelly* ⁓

6 half-pint jars

2 cups fruit juice or water
1 cup fresh herbs
2 tablespoons lemon juice
3½ cups sugar
Few drops food coloring (optional)
1 pouch liquid pectin
6 fresh herb sprigs (optional)

1. Begin preheating water in the boiling water bath canner and tea kettle. Sterilize half-pint jars and prepare lids.
2. In a covered saucepan, combine the fruit juice or water with the herbs. Heat to the boiling point, but do not boil. Remove from the heat and let steep, covered, for 20 minutes. Strain the liquid through a coffee filter paper or jelly bag, squeezing the herbs left in the paper or bag to extract all flavor. Discard the herbs.
3. In a large saucepan, combine the herb infusion, lemon juice, sugar, and food coloring. Bring to a full rolling boil over high heat, stirring constantly.
4. When the boil cannot be stirred down, pour in the pectin, stirring constantly. Boil for 1 minute. Remove from the heat. Stir and skim off any foam that collects on top.
5. Add 1 herb sprig to each sterilized jar. Immediately pour in the hot jelly, leaving ¼-inch headspace. Seal.
6. Process in a boiling water bath for 5 minutes.

Preserving Each Herb

Anise

Harvest anise seed when it begins to dry on the plant. Dry seed stalks in dehydrator at 110°F for 10 to 12 hours, or in a conventional oven at 110°F for 18 to 24 hours, or outdoors out of direct sunlight for several days. Remove seeds, discard stalks, and store.

Uses. Use licorice-flavored seeds in herb teas and baking.

Basil

Snip leaves from stems of sweet basil as soon as they have developed. Wash and pat dry. Dry leaves in dehydrator or oven at 110°F for 8 to 12 hours. Dry stems outdoors for 1 to 2 days.

Uses. In cooking, especially Italian dishes and with tomatoes, fish, cheese, and eggs. Delicious in herbal vinegars and jelly.

Chervil

Pick small bunches from immature plants. Dry in dehydrator or oven at 110°F for 12 to 18 hours, or outdoors out of direct sunlight for several days. Crumble leaves, discard stems, and store.

Uses. To flavor egg and cheese dishes.

Chives

Harvest chives before flowers form. Their flavor is retained best by freezing by one of the methods detailed above. Or chop stems and dry in dehydrator or oven at 110 ° F for 4 to 6 hours, or outdoors out of direct sunlight for 8 to 10 hours. Store.

Uses. In soups, salads, casseroles, sauces, and as a garnish. In herbal vinegars and jellies.

Dill

Harvest dill for leaves when the plants are immature. Harvest heads as soon as flower buds form, but before all the buds are open. Dill heads can be bagged and frozen for use in pickles. Fresh dill weed can be frozen by any of the methods listed above. Dry finely chopped leaves in dehydrator or conventional oven at 110°F for 6 to 8 hours; dry seeds for 4 to 6 hours at 120°F. Dry stems outdoors for 3 to 4 days. Dry seeds on trays outdoors in direct sun for 4 to 6 hours.

Uses. To flavor egg, fish, and cheese dishes. In pickles and fresh salads. Makes excellent vinegar.

Fennel

Pick immature fennel leaves in the morning after the dew has dried. Fennel seed is harvested after it has dried somewhat in the pod, but before the seed pods burst. Freeze leaves by any of the methods listed above. Dry finely chopped leaves in dehydrator or conventional oven at 110°F for 6 to 8 hours; dry seeds for 4 to 6 hours at 120°F. Dry stems outdoors for 3 to 4 days. Dry seeds on trays outdoors in direct sun for 4 to 6 hours.
Uses. In baked goods. Seeds, in herb teas.

Marjoram

Pick the leaves at maturity. Dry leaves in dehydrator or conventional oven at 110°F for 6 to 8 hours. Dry leaves outdoors out of direct sunlight for 8 to 12 hours.
Uses. In cooking, especially with meat. In bouquet garni.

Mint

Pick the leaves in early summer, when leaves are most fragrant. Dry leaves in dehydrator or conventional oven at 110°F for 6 to 8 hours. Dry outdoors for 8 to 12 hours. Or freeze by any of the methods listed above.
Uses. Delightful in teas, jellies, with vegetables, and in desserts.

Oregano

Pick the leaves just as the flowers open. Dry leaves in dehydrator at 110°F for 4 to 8 hours or in a conventional oven at 110°F for 6 to 8 hours. Dry leaves outdoors out of direct sunlight for 8 to 12 hours.
Uses. In cooking, especially with Italian dishes, meats. In seasonings mixes.

Parsley

Cut parsley tops with scissors as soon as new leaves have formed and harvest throughout the season. You can freeze whole sprigs or finely chopped leaves by any of the methods explained above. Dry sprigs in dehydrator at 110°F for 8 to 12 hours or chopped leaves for 6 to 8 hours. Or dry in a conventional oven at 110°F for 8 to 12 hours. Dry leaves outdoors out of direct sunlight for 8 to 12 hours.
Uses. In cooking, in bouquet garni, and as a garnish.

Rosemary

Harvest young leaves as soon as the aroma has developed. Dry leaves in dehydrator at 110°F for 6 to 8 hours or chopped leaves for 6 to 8 hours. Or dry in a conventional oven at 110°F for 8 to 12 hours. Dry leaves outdoors out of direct sunlight for 8 to 10 hours.

Uses. In cooking, especially with meats. In teas and hair rinses.

Sage

Pick the leaves at maturity. Dry leaves in dehydrator at 110°F for 8 to 12 hours. Dry leaves in a conventional oven at 110°F for 10 to 12 hours. Or dry leaves outdoors out of direct sunlight for 10 to 14 hours.

Uses. In cooking, especially with sausage, cheese, and poultry. Also in teas.

Tarragon

Pick the leaves when the plants are young. Dry the leaves in dehydrator at 110°F for 6 to 8 hours. Dry leaves in a conventional oven at 110°F in an oven for 8 to 12 hours. Or dry leaves outdoors out of direct sunlight for 8 to 12 hours.

Uses. In cooking, especially with tomato dishes, and poultry. Also to flavor vinegar and in herbal jellies.

Thyme

Pick the leaves when the plants first begin to flower. Dry the leaves in dehydrator or conventional oven at 110°F for 6 to 8 hours. Or dry leaves outdoors out of direct sunlight for 8 to 12 hours.

Uses. In cooking, especially with Italian dishes, meats, stews, wild game. Also to flavor teas and vinegar, and in herbal jellies.

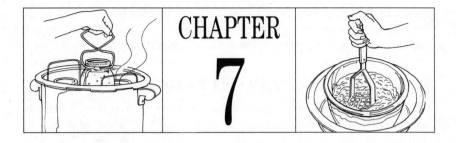

Pickles, Relishes, Sauerkraut, and Sauces

VARIETY IS THE SPICE OF OUR LIFE, and pickles and relishes spice up many of my home-cooked meals.

There are many books on pickles and relishes, but this one has been written for the busy person. The recipes were chosen to be both speedy and practical. I have tried to find shortcuts to reduce work time. One shortcut discovery I am very proud of is my "Busy Person's Relish-Sauce-Chutney" recipe (page 129). I found that I could make an Indian relish, can half of it, and save half. To the half I saved, I added peach preserves to make a great tasting sweet-and-sour sauce. I canned half of that. To the half remaining, I added nuts and raisins and ended up with a marvelous chutney (so good I like to eat it right out of the jar!). Three different sauces out of one basic recipe — that's the kind of shortcut I hope you'll experiment with in your kitchen.

Pickles

Traditionally there have been three basic methods of making pickles: brining in salt, used most commonly for dill pickles and sauerkraut; fresh-pack, quick-processed pickles, which can turn vegetables into spicy sweet or sour pickles; and relishes, made by chopping or grinding a mixture of vegetables, adding seasonings, vinegar, and sweeteners, and cooking to the desired consistency. New to picklers are freezer pickles. These are the easiest to make, but if your freezer space is at a premium, you will find the other recipes in this section are quick and easy to make as well.

Basic Ingredients for Making Pickles

Vegetables and Fruit. These should be blemish-free, firm, and fresh. Small slender cucumbers and zucchini make the best whole pickles. Medium-size cucumbers or zucchini make good sliced pickles. Larger vegetables that have gone past their prime can be used to make relishes and sauces. Do not use waxed cucumbers; brine cannot penetrate the wax coating. Be sure to remove all blossom ends from the cucumbers; otherwise an enzyme in these blossoms may cause the pickles to soften during fermentation.

Salt. Use pure coarse salt, pickling salt, or kosher salt. Iodized salt will darken pickles and should not be used.

Vinegar. Use a high-quality vinegar of at least 4 to 6 percent acidity. (Don't use homemade vinegars.) Cider vinegar gives pickles a mellow, fruity taste and will produce a darker pickle. While distilled vinegar gives a sharper, more acid taste, it is best to use if you want light-colored pickles. Never reduce the amount of vinegar called for in a recipe. Weakening the vinegar could enable bacteria to grow in the brine. If a less sour taste is desired, add additional sweetener.

Sweeteners. Use either white or brown sugar, or honey. Brown sugar will produce a darker pickle. Honey usually will cloud the brine.

Spices. Use only fresh spices. Old spices may cause the pickles to taste musty. Whole spices are recommended over powdered. The whole spices should be loosely tied in a cheesecloth or small muslin bag and removed from the brine before packing the pickles in jars to prevent discoloration. However, many of the best cooks I know put the spices right into the brine and pack them with the pickles. The flavor of the spice is stronger, and the color is darker, but not unpleasantly so.

Firming Agents. In the old days, many cooks used alum or grape leaves added to the brine or packed in the jar to produce a crisp pickle. These firming agents aren't necessary if fresh produce is used and recipes are followed carefully.

Equipment

The equipment needed for making pickles is similar to that required for canning. Do not use copper, brass, galvanized, or iron or aluminum pots or utensils. These metals will react with the acids and salt used in pickles, causing color and taste changes.

Here is the list of equipment you will need: sharp paring knives, scrub brush, large bowls, measuring cups and spoons, colander, fine sieves, cheesecloth, cutting board, crocks or large glass jars, heavy plate, clean jars, steam or boiling water bath canner, preserving kettle or large roaster, pan containing screw bands and lids in hot water, wide-mouth funnel, ladle, large wooden and slotted spoons, timer, hot pads, heavy bath towels, jar lifter, nonmetallic spatula for expelling bubbles from jars.

Before you start making pickles, be sure your work area and all equipment are spotlessly clean. If your jars have not been prewashed, wash them. Check the jars for nicks and cracks.

Processing

The USDA recommends that all pickles be processed in a boiling water bath for long-term storage. If you feel that processing alters the texture of your pickles, then you may keep unprocessed pickles in the refrigerator for a few weeks. I definitely do not recommend storing unprocessed pickles on a shelf.

Step-by-Step Pickle Making

1. Preheat the canner, jars, and lids while preparing the recipe. To preheat a boiling water bath canner, fill the boiling water bath canner with 4 to 4½ inches of hot tap water. Set the jars on a rack inside the canner, bottom sides up. Turn the heat on high. Leave the jars in the hot water until needed. Prepare the lids according to the manufacturer's directions.

2. Wash your vegetables thoroughly.

3. Prepare the vegetables according to the recipe directions — dice, chop, slice, and so on.

4. Add seasonings, sweeteners, and vinegar to the vegetables, according to the recipe directions.

5. Cook, if necessary.

6. Pack the vegetables firmly in the hot jars, making sure that the pickling brine fills the jars to the

Heat filled canner.

Preheat lids.

Add brine.

Lower jar into canner.

level indicated in the recipe.

7. Release any air bubbles in the jar by inserting the spatula and running it between the contents and the side of the jar.

8. Add more brine, if needed to maintain proper headspace.

9. Wipe the rim of the jar with a clean, damp cloth to remove any food particles, seeds, or spices.

10. Adjust the lids as the manufacturer recommends.

11. Place the filled jars on a rack in the preheated boiling water bath canner. Make sure the water covers the jars by at least 2 inches. Cover the canner and bring the water to a boil.

12. Process for the length of time indicated in the individual recipe. Make sure the water is boiling throughout the processing time.

13. When the processing time is up, carefully remove the jars from the canner, using a jar lifter.

14. Cool the jars for 24 hours. Check the seal. Any jars not sealed should be refrigerated immediately and used within 2 weeks.

15. Remove screw bands, wipe sealed jars, label, date, and store in a cool, dry, dark place.

Pickles should be chilled before serving.

When opening each new jar, check for signs of spoilage: bulging lids, leakage, mold, bad odor, very soft or mushy pickles. If there is the slightest doubt in your mind, *do not taste.* Dispose of the pickles where no person or animal can be harmed by them. Wash and sterilize the jar before storing or reusing.

Recipes

Be sure to read through each recipe before beginning, so you know whether you have time for the recipe. Some require leaving the vegetables in a salt brine for as little as an hour or as much as 10 days.

TIP *Prewash your jars and make up the pickling brine ahead. Heat the brine and can the dills as they come along, 2 or 3 quarts at a time.*

∽ Short-Brine Kosher Dill Pickles ∽

7 quarts

6	tablespoons pickling salt
4	tablespoons sugar
6	cups cider vinegar
6	cups water
7	large grape leaves (optional)
2	tablespoons mixed pickling spices
16–17	pounds pickling cucumbers (3 to 5 inches long)
21	large dill heads or 7 tablespoons dill seed
14	cloves of garlic
7	whole cayenne peppers (dried)

1. Preheat hot tap water in canner. Prepare quart jars and lids. In a saucepan, mix the salt, sugar, vinegar, water, grape leaves. Add the whole pickling spices tied in a spice bag. Heat to boiling. Meanwhile, scrub the cucumbers.
2. Place 3 dill heads (or 1 tablespoon dill seed), 2 cloves garlic, and 1 cayenne pepper in each jar. Pack the cucumbers in the jars.
3. Fill the jars with hot brine to cover the cucumbers. Place 1 grape leaf in each jar. Leave ½-inch headspace.
4. Process for 15 minutes once water returns to a boil.
5. Cool sealed jars. Check seals. Remove screw bands. Label. Store.

∽ *Sour Pickles* ∽

7 to 8 pints

Larger, slender cucumbers can be used for this recipe, but they should be cut in small chunks or spears.

2	quarts cider vinegar
½	cup dry mustard
½	cup sugar
½	cup pickling salt
60–80	scrubbed tiny cucumbers (1½ to 2½ inches long)

1. Combine the vinegar, mustard, sugar, salt. Pour into a clean gallon jar or container.
2. Add the cucumbers. Let stand for 7 days in a cool place.
3. Preheat hot tap water in the canner; prepare the jars and lids. Meanwhile, drain the pickles and save the brine. Pack the pickles in clean jars. Fill the jars with the saved brine to cover the pickles. Leave ½-inch headspace.
4. Process for 10 minutes in the preheated boiling water bath canner. Start counting time as soon as water returns to boiling.
5. Cool sealed jars. Check seals. Remove screw bands. Label. Store.

TIP *If you do not have enough small pickles for a full batch, pick the cucumbers daily as they come along and add to the brine. After each gallon jar is filled, let it stand 7 days before processing in pints. Process pints for 10 minutes.*

∼ *Quick Dill Pickles* ∼

3 quarts

3 cups white vinegar

3 cups water

⅓ cup pickling salt

4 pounds cucumbers, washed and cut into spears

6 heads dill or 6 tablespoons dill seed

3 peeled cloves garlic (optional)

9 peppercorns

1. Combine liquids and salt, and heat to boiling.

2. Pack cucumbers into hot, clean quart jars. Add to each jar 2 heads dill or 2 tablespoons dill seed, 1 clove garlic, and 3 peppercorns.

3. Fill the jars with the hot pickling syrup, leaving ½ inch of headroom. Adjust lids.

4. Process in a boiling water bath for 20 minutes. For the best flavor, let the pickles stand and mellow for several weeks before eating.

Excerpted from *Keeping the Harvest*, by Nancy Chioffi and Gretchen Mead (Storey Publishing).

⌒ *Sweet Chunk Pickles* ⌒

4 pints

8	cucumbers, 5 inches long
½	cup pickling salt (approximately)
1	quart cold water (approximately)
4	cups white vinegar
4	cups water
2	large grape leaves (optional)
4	cups sugar
1	tablespoon mixed pickling spices

1. Scrub the cucumbers. Cover with cold salt brine made of ½ cup salt for each quart of cold water used.
2. Let the cucumbers stand for 3 days.
3. Drain. Cover with cold water. Let stand for 24 hours.
4. Drain. Cover with cold water. Let stand for another 24 hours.
5. Drain. Cover with cold water. Let stand for another 24 hours.
6. Combine 2 cups vinegar, 4 cups water, and grape leaves. Heat to boiling. Meanwhile, cut the cucumbers into ½-inch chunks. Pour the hot brine over the cucumbers.
7. Let stand for 2 days.
8. Drain. Discard brine and grape leaves. Combine sugar, 2 cups vinegar, and spices. Heat to boiling. Pour over chunks.
9. Let stand for 24 hours.
10. Pour off brine and heat to boiling. Pour over chunks.
11. Let stand for 24 hours. Repeat step 10. Let stand 24 hours.
12. Fill canner with hot tap water. Preheat water and jars in canner. Prepare lids. Meanwhile reheat brine to boiling.
13. Pack the jars with pickles. Fill with hot brine. Leave ½-inch headspace.
14. Place jars in preheated canner. Process for 10 minutes once water has returned to a boil.
15. Cool jars. Check seals. Remove screw bands. Label. Store.

∽ *Sunshine Pickles* ∽

7 pints

3 cups sugar
3 cups cider vinegar
1 tablespoon pickling salt
1 tablespoon celery seed
3 large grape leaves (optional)
5 quarts peeled and seeded ripe cucumbers or
   zucchinis (10 firm cucumbers or zucchinis,
   6 to 8 inches long)
4 large onions, sliced
1 tablespoon turmeric

1. Combine the sugar, vinegar, salt, celery seed, and grape leaves in a preserving kettle. Heat on low while preparing cucumbers.
2. Peel and seed cucumbers; cut into "tongues" (2½- to 3-inch slices). Peel and slice the onions.
3. Place the vegetables in the hot brine. Bring to a boil, simmer until translucent. Meanwhile, fill the canner with hot tap water. Preheat jars and water in canner and prepare lids.
4. Remove the grape leaves; add the turmeric. Stir well. Pack the pickles in jars. Leave ½-inch headspace. (If pickling zucchinis, add ⅓ grape leaf to each jar.)
5. Place the filled jars in preheated canner. Process for 10 minutes once water has returned to a boil.
6. Cool jars. Check seal. Remove screw bands. Label. Store.

～ *Freezer Pickles* ～

4 pints

> 2   quarts sliced cucumbers
>   (approximately 30 cucumbers, 5 inches long)
> 2   medium onions
> 2   tablespoons pickling salt
> 1½   cups sugar
> 1   cup cider vinegar
> 1   teaspoon celery seed

1. Scrub and slice the cucumbers. Peel and thinly slice the onions. Sprinkle with salt. Mix well.
2. Cover bowl and let stand for 3 hours.
3. Rinse the vegetables with cold tap water, and drain thoroughly. Meanwhile, mix sugar, vinegar, celery seed.
4. Pour the brine over the vegetables. Mix, cover. Refrigerate overnight.
5. Pack the pickles in straight-sided containers. Cover with brine. Leave 1-inch headspace. Seal. Freeze. Defrost in the refrigerator for 8 hours before serving.

∼ *Freezer Coleslaw* ∼

Approximately 4 pints

1   medium-size cabbage
1   carrot
1   green pepper
2   tablespoons pickling salt
1   cup cider vinegar
1¼ cups sugar
¼   cup water
1   teaspoon celery seed

1. Shred the cabbage, carrot, green pepper. Sprinkle with salt; mix well. Cover. Let stand for 1 hour.
2. Meanwhile, mix the vinegar, sugar, water, celery seed. Bring to a boil. Boil 1 minute.
3. Rinse the vegetables with cold tap water and drain. Squeeze out as much water as possible.
4. Pour the brine over the cabbage mixture. Stir well. Cool.
5. Pack in straight-sided containers. Leave 1-inch head space. Seal. Freeze. Defrost and store in refrigerator before serving.

∼ *Pickled Beets* ∼

7 pints

10–12	pounds beets (without tops)
1	quart cider vinegar
⅔	cup sugar
1	cup water
2	tablespoons salt

1. Cut the tops and roots off flush with the beet. Scrub thoroughly.
2. Place the beets on a rack in a large roaster. Cover and bake at 400°F until tender, about 1 hour for medium-size beets. Meanwhile, preheat hot tap water and jars in canner. Prepare lids.
3. In a saucepan, mix the vinegar, sugar, water, salt. Heat to boiling.
4. When the beets are tender, fill the roaster with cold water. Slip the skins of the beets.
5. Pack the beets in hot jars, whole or cut. Add brine to cover. Leave ½-inch headspace.
6. Put filled jars in the preheated canner. Process for 30 minutes once water has returned to a boil.
7. Cool jars. Check seals. Remove screw bands. Label. Store.

∾ *Dilly Beans* ∾

4 pints

2½ cups vinegar
2½ cups water
¼ cup salt
2 pounds green beans, trimmed
1 teaspoon cayenne pepper
4 cloves garlic
4 heads dill

1. Preheat hot tap water in canner and tea kettle. Prepare lids. Sterilize pint-size canning jars.
2. In a saucepan, mix the vinegar, water, and salt. Heat to boiling.
3. Pack the beans in hot jars, leaving ½-inch headspace. To each pint, add ¼ teaspoon cayenne, 1 clove garlic, and 1 head dill. Pour hot liquid of beans, leaving ¼-inch headspace.
4. Put filled jars in the preheated canner. Process for 5 minutes once water has returned to a boil.
5. Cool jars. Check seals. Remove screw bands. Label. Store.

∽ *German Pickle Relish* ∽

Approximately 7 pints

2	quarts finely chopped or ground cabbage
1	quart ground green tomatoes
2	sweet red peppers
1	quart sliced onions
1	tablespoon celery seed
1	tablespoon pickling salt
¼	teaspoon pepper
12	whole cloves
½	cup mustard seed
4½	cups sugar
1	quart cider vinegar
1	teaspoon turmeric

1. Finely chop or grind the cabbage, green tomatoes, peppers, onions.
2. Combine the vegetables with the remaining ingredients, *except* turmeric, in a large saucepan. Heat to boiling. Simmer until cabbage is well done (about 1 hour). Meanwhile, preheat hot tap water and jars in canner. Prepare lids.
3. Remove relish from heat when done. Stir in turmeric.
4. Pack the relish in hot jars. Leave 1-inch headspace.
5. Put filled jars in preheated canner. Turn heat on high. Process for 10 minutes once water has returned to a boil.
6. Cool jars. Check seals. Remove screw bands. Label. Store.

~ *Busy Person's Relish-Sauce-Chutney* ~

14 pints and 7 half-pints

This recipe makes three great tasting sauces: Indian Relish, a spicy sauce to eat with meats (makes a great Thousand Island Salad Dressing); Sweet-and-Sour Sauce, to use with meat, poultry, and seafood (especially good with Chinese or Polynesian dishes); and Chutney, fantastic with everything. It's very easy to make, but takes a little longer than other recipes. This is a good project for a free day.

Relish:

4	quarts tomato puree (approximately 24 large tomatoes)
24	large apples
7	cups chopped onions (approximately 18 large onions)
2	quarts cider vinegar
6	cups sugar
⅔	cup salt
2	teaspoons ground cloves
2	teaspoons red pepper
2	teaspoons cinnamon
2	teaspoons dry mustard

Sweet-and-Sour Additions:

7	cups peach preserves
2	teaspoons garlic powder
1	teaspoon Tabasco sauce

Chutney Additions:

1	cup raisins
1	cup chopped walnuts

1. Puree tomatoes in a hand-cranked strainer. Peel, core, and coarsely chop apples. Peel and chop onions. Mix in large roaster or preserving kettle with vinegar, sugar, salt, cloves, red pepper, cinnamon, dry mustard.

2. Bring to a boil and simmer until thick, about 2 hours. Meanwhile, preheat hot tap water and jars in canner. Prepare lids.

3. Ladle hot sauce into 7 hot pint-size jars. Leave ½-inch headspace.

4. Put filled jars in the preheated canner. Turn heat on high. Process for 10 minutes once water has returned to a boil. While the jars are processing, add the peach preserves to the remaining sauce and reheat to boiling.

5. Fill 7 pint-size jars, leaving ½-inch headspace.

6. Put filled jars in the preheated canner. Turn heat on high. Process the jars for 10 minutes once water returns to a boil. While the jars are processing, add the raisins and nuts to the remaining sauce, and reheat to boiling.

7. Pack the remaining hot sauce into 7 ½-pint jars. Leave ½-inch headspace.

8. Put filled jars into the preheated canner. Turn heat on high. Process for 10 minutes once water returns to a boil.

9. Cool jars. Check seals, remove screw bands. Label. Store.

∿ *Zucchini Relish* ∿

Approximately 7 pints

10   cups finely chopped zucchini
4   cups finely chopped onions
1   green pepper, chopped finely
1   red pepper (sweet), chopped finely
5   tablespoons pickling salt
2½   cups white vinegar
1   large cayenne pepper with seeds
1   tablespoon nutmeg
1   tablespoon dry mustard
1   tablespoon turmeric
1   tablespoon cornstarch
½   teaspoon pepper
2   teaspoons celery salt
4½   cups sugar

1. Chop the vegetables and sprinkle salt over them. Mix well. Let stand overnight.
2. Drain the vegetables. Rinse thoroughly with cold tap water. Drain again.
3. Place the vegetables in a large kettle with the remaining ingredients. (Puree the cayenne pepper in blender with a little of the vinegar for better flavor.) Bring to a boil. Simmer for 30 to 45 minutes until thick. Meanwhile preheat hot tap water and jars in canner. Prepare lids.
4. Pack jars. Leave ½-inch headspace.
5. Put filled jars in preheated canner. Process for 10 minutes once water has returned to a boil.
6. Cool jars. Check seals. Remove screw bands. Label. Store.

∽ *Sauerkraut* ∽

7 pints

5   pounds cabbage
3   tablespoons pickling salt
12   juniper berries
½   cup Chablis wine

1. Shred the cabbage. Layer the cabbage, salt, and 3 juniper berries per layer in a large crock or bowl that holds at least 1 gallon. Tap every other layer with a potato masher to get rid of trapped air bubbles. Cover with a clean cloth and weigh down with a heavy plate. Place this container in another pan to collect fermenting juices that overflow. Place in an area that remains between 65° and 75°F.

Tap with masher.

2. By the next day, brine will form and cover the cabbage. By the second day, scum will start to form. On the second day, pour the wine over all.

Cover with cloth.

Weight down.

Rinse the plate and cloth and replace each day.

3. Skim any scum that has formed after 2 weeks.

4. Skim again after 4 weeks.

5. To can (hot pack only), fill the canner with hot tap water and preheat water in jars in canner. Prepare lids.

   While the canner and jars are preheating, heat the sauerkraut to simmer. *Do not boil.* Pack in hot jars. Leave ½-inch headspace. If you run short of juice, mix a brine of 1½ tablespoons salt to 1 quart boiling water. (Divide this mixture between the jars; do not use the new brine to fill just 1 jar.)

6. Put filled jars in the preheated canner. Process: 10 minutes for pints, 15 minutes for quarts, once water has returned to a boil.

7. Cool jars. Check seals. Remove screw bands. Label. Store.

Sauerkraut can be stored in a crock, and not canned, if the area in which it is stored remains at a constant 38°F. When removing a portion of sauerkraut from the crock, make sure the remaining sauerkraut is covered with brine. Mix more brine, 1½ tablespoons of pickling salt to 1 quart water, if necessary. Always use a glass or china cup to remove a portion of sauerkraut.

How can you tell if sauerkraut is spoiled? Spoiled sauerkraut has an off odor and changes in color. Soft kraut is caused by insufficient salt, uneven distribution of salt, temperature too high during fermentation, or not expelling air bubbles when packing. Pink kraut indicates a yeast growth on the surface, too much or improperly distributed salt, or not keeping the kraut weighted down during fermentation. Rotted kraut is caused by an insufficient covering of brine to exclude air. Dark kraut is caused by cabbage that was washed or trimmed improperly; insufficient covering of brine to exclude air; poor distribution of salt; high fermentation, processing, or storage temperatures; or kraut that has been in storage too long.

∼ *Spicy Salsa* ∼

About 7 pints

5 pounds tomatoes

2 pounds hot chili peppers

1 pound onion, chopped

1 cup vinegar

3 teaspoons salt

½ teaspoon pepper

1. Fill canner with hot tap water and preheat water and jars in canner. Prepare lids.
2. Puree tomatoes in a hand-cranked strainer. Chop chili peppers and onions finely. Put all the ingredients in a large saucepan. Bring to a boil, then simmer for 10 minutes.
3. Ladle the hot sauce into hot jars. Leave ½-inch headspace.
4. Put the filled jars in the preheated canner. Process pints for 15 minutes once water has returned to a boil.
5. Cool jars. Check seals. Label. Store.

TIP *You can also cook this sauce on the top of the stove. Place a small, clean window screen over your roaster to prevent spatters. This will save clean-up time later.*

∼ *Kate's Fresh Salsa* ∼

Makes 2 cups

2   large tomatoes, chopped and seeded
1   medium Vidalia or sweet onion, chopped
2   tablespoons lime juice (2 limes)
⅓   cup chopped fresh cilantro
2   tablespoons chopped green chilies
2   drops Tabasco sauce
    Salt and freshly ground pepper, to taste

1. Mix all ingredients in a medium-size bowl. Let stand for 30 minutes to blend the flavors.
2. If you make the salsa ahead of time, leave out the chilies until just before serving.

Excerpted from *Weekend!*, by Edith Stovel and Pamela Wakefield (Storey Publishing).

～ *Just Like Store-Bought Catsup* ～

12 pints

8	quarts tomato puree (approximately 24 pounds tomatoes)
12	ounces thick tomato paste
3	green peppers
5	large onions
2	cups cider vinegar
1	cup light corn syrup
1	cup sugar
1	teaspoon pepper
2	tablespoons salt
2	teaspoons allspice

1. Puree the tomatoes with a hand-cranked strainer. Liquefy the tomato paste, peppers, and onions in a blender with some of the vinegar. Mix the purees with remaining ingredients in a large roaster. Stir well. Bring to a boil on top of the stove.
2. Cook, uncovered, in a 200°F oven for 10 hours. Do not stir.
3. One hour before cooking time is up, fill canner with hot tap water and preheat water and jars in canner. Prepare lids.
4. When cooking time is up, ladle the hot catsup into the hot pint jars. Leave ½-inch headspace.
5. Put the filled jars in the preheated canner. Turn heat on high. Process pints for 15 minutes once water has returned to a boil.
6. Cool jars. Check seals. Remove screw bands. Label. Store.

TIP Spaghetti sauce and catsup can be reduced on top of the stove by cooking for 3 hours, but you must stir often to avoid boiling over or sticking. Sauces cooked in the oven take longer to reduce; they do not need to be stirred. They will not boil over, nor will they stick to the pot. To hurry the process toward the end, you can quickly reduce the sauce by cooking it for a very short period of time on top of the stove.

∽ *Jan's Spicy Spaghetti Sauce* ∽

6 to 7 quarts

10	quarts tomato puree (approximately 30 pounds tomatoes)
4	large onions
⅓	cup dried sweet basil
2	tablespoons dried oregano
1	teaspoon dried thyme
1	teaspoon pepper
¾	cup honey or sugar (optional)
1	teaspoon dried marjoram
5	bay leaves
1	tablespoon crushed red pepper
1	tablespoon garlic powder
2	tablespoons salt
1½	tablespoons dried parsley

1. Puree tomatoes in a hand-cranked strainer. Chop onion finely. Put the vegetables with remaining ingredients in a large roaster. Stir well. Bring to a boil on top of the stove.
2. Cook, uncovered, in a 200°F oven for 10 hours. Do not stir.
3. One hour before cooking time is up, fill canner with hot tap water and preheat water and jars in canner. Prepare lids.
4. When cooking time is up, ladle the hot sauce into hot jars. Leave ½-inch headspace. Add ½ teaspoon citric acid to each jar to ensure the safety of the sauce.
5. Put the filled jars in the preheated canner. Process: 35 minutes for pints and quarts, once water has returned to a boil.
6. Cool jars. Check seals. Label. Store.

TIP   *Citric acid is added to seasoned tomato sauces to guarantee that the sauce is acidic enough to be canned safely in a boiling water bath. Citric acid is available from your drugstore and will not affect the flavor of the sauce. Instead of citric acid, you can use 2 tablespoons of bottled lemon juice per quart of sauce.*

10 Commonly Asked Pickling Questions

Must I process pickles and relishes?

Yes. The USDA now recommends processing all pickles and relishes to ensure destruction of harmful bacteria.

Must I sterilize jars when I process pickles and relishes?

To process pickles and relishes, it is not necessary to sterilize jars, if you process for 10 minutes or more in a boiling water bath.

What causes soft or slippery pickles?

Not using freshly picked cucumbers, too little salt in the brine, acidity of vinegar is less than 5 percent, reducing the acid strength of the vinegar by adding more water than the recipe called for, not removing scum regularly, vegetables not covered with brine, hard water, not removing blossom ends from cucumbers, processing too long, or storing pickles where it is too warm.

What causes hollow pickles?

Growing conditions (long dry spells followed by heavy rains), cucumbers stored too long before pickling, brine not strong enough, or high fermentation temperatures.

What causes shriveled pickles?

Cucumbers stored too long before pickling, pickling solution too sweet or vinegar too strong, not enough salt in the brine, cooking too long, or processing too long.

What causes dark pickles?

Using too much spice, not removing whole spices from brine before packing pickles, minerals in the water (hard water), overcooking, cooking in an iron kettle, using iodized salt, or low nitrogen content of cucumbers.

Why do my pickles become dull or faded?

Poor quality cucumbers, sunburned or overmature cucumbers, or poor growing conditions.

What is the white sediment that collects in the bottom of my jars of pickles?

Bacteria caused by fermentation, fluctuations in storage temperatures, or not using pure canning salt. It is usually not harmful unless the pickles are spoiled. If the pickles are spoiled, the jars frequently will spurt liquid when opened.

What causes pickles to spoil?

Not following directions carefully for packing and processing, using ingredients that are too old, or weakening the vinegar solution by adding more water than the recipe called for.

When I add whole garlic to my dills the garlic turns blue. Why?

Hard water is usually the cause.

CHAPTER

8

Jams, Jellies, Preserves, and Marmalades

IF THE IDEA OF SLAVING over a hot preserving kettle doesn't sound like fun, relax. There are many easy ways to enjoy making jams and jellies, and they don't all involve working long hours in a hot kitchen.

Freezer jams and jellies take much of the work out of preserving. These involve very little cooking — just enough to allow the pectin mixture and sugar to dissolve in the fruit juice. Another trick is to save your jam- and jelly-making for later in the season, when the weather has cooled down. You can make preserves from frozen or canned fruit, instead of fresh.

One shortcut you cannot take is to double a batch — the preserve probably won't gel properly. When making preserves, it is important to follow the recipe carefully and accurately. If you are using a commercial pectin, then accurate measuring and timing are critical; if you are making a preserve without added pectin, then using a thermometer to gauge when the product has reached the gel point is safest.

If you are new to making preserves, start by making jams with added pectin. They are easy and fairly fail-safe. Graduate to making jams and other preserves without added pectin.

If all you want is a satisfactory spread to go with peanut butter and another good way to preserve your fruit harvest, there is no need to go beyond jams. I include jelly-making here because sometimes you just want to have jelly. But be forewarned — the process is more time-consuming. I recommend using commercial pectin when making jelly, as there are many pitfalls along the way without it.

Types of Preserves

Basically there are six types of jellied fruit products — all called preserves. *Jellies* are usually made by cooking clear fruit juice with sugar. They should hold their shape on a spoon but be soft enough to spread on toast. *Jams* are thick, sweet spreads made from cooked and crushed fruit and sugar. They are less firm than jelly. *Preserves* are made with small pieces of fruit suspended in a clear, slightly gelled syrup. *Conserves* are jams that are made from fruit combinations. Sometimes they contain raisins, nuts, or coconut. *Marmalades* are soft fruit jellies that contain small pieces of fruit or peel evenly suspended in a clear jelly. *Butters* are fruit pulp cooked down to a spreading consistency.

Ingredients for Making Preserves

Fruit. Fruit forms the basis of most preserves. They don't have to be picture-perfect specimens since they will be cut up, mashed, or made into juice. But the fruit should be of high quality and free from mold or any spoilage. You can make preserves from fresh, frozen, or canned fruit. If you are using frozen or canned fruit, be sure to take into account the sugar already added to the fruit. For the best results, it is safer to use unsweetened fruit.

Most fruits (with the notable exception of berries) can be held at room temperature for several days if you can't preserve right away.

Pectin. Pectin is a substance that occurs naturally in fruit; it is what causes fruit juice to gel. Some fruits — most apples, grapes, blueberries, blackberries, cherries, cranberries, grapes — have enough natural pectin to make high-quality preserves. Others require the addition of pectin to form a good gel. Commercial pectins are made from apples or citrus fruit and are available in both powdered and liquid forms. Be sure to follow the manufacturer's directions or tested recipes when using commercial pectin. The powdered and liquid forms are not interchangeable.

It may seem more "natural" to avoid using these commercial pectins — to make jams and jellies the old-fashioned way by cooking down fruit and sugar until you have a thick preserve — but I recommend them for busy people for several reasons. First, fully ripe fruit can be used with these products, so when you harvest or when you get around to making your preserves is less critical. Second, cooking time is considerably shorter. Third, there is no guesswork involved in terms of when the product is done. And finally, the yield is greater — more jars for your effort. If you have found that commercial pectins make a preserve that is too sweet for your taste, try one of the reduced-sugar pectins on the market.

Sugar. Sugar is an important ingredient in preserves. It must be present in the right amount (along with some acid) to activate the pectin. It also acts as a preservative. If you reduce the amount of sugar in a recipe, you will probably not get a good gel. White sugar is the best sweetener for preserves, as it contributes sweetness without flavor. You can try using part honey or part corn syrup instead, but I don't recommend brown sugar or maple syrup as they contribute too much flavor.

Acid. Acid is needed for both gelling and flavor. The acidity of fruit varies and is higher in underripe fruit. Most recipes call for the addition of lemon juice. Although the quantity is small, don't omit it.

Equipment

The equipment needed for making preserves is similar to that required for canning. Do not use aluminum, brass, galvanized, or iron pots or utensils. These metals will react with the fruit, causing color and taste changes.

In addition to the boiling water bath, you will need a large saucepan that will hold 8 to 10 quarts, with a heavy bottom to prevent scorching and tall sides to prevent the mixture from boiling over. A jelly bag or suitable cloth is needed for extracting juice for jellies. A candy, jelly, or deep-fat thermometer is needed if you are making preserves without added pectin; if you are using commercial pectin, you will need a timer or a clock with a second hand.

Processing

Unless you plan to store your preserves in the refrigerator or freezer, you will need to use sterilized jars and to process the jars in a boiling water bath for 5 minutes.

Step-by-Step Jam- and Preserve-Making (No Added Pectin)

1. Preheat the canner, sterilize jars, and prepare lids while preparing the recipe.

To preheat a boiling water bath canner, fill the boiling water bath canner with 4 to 4½ inches of hot tap water. Set the jars on a rack inside the canner, bottom sides up. Turn the heat on high and bring to a boil. Boil for 10 minutes. Turn off the heat but leave the jars in the water until needed.

Wash and rinse all canning lids and screw bands. Treat the lids as directed by the manufacturer. Remember that lids can be used only once.

2. Wash your fruit thoroughly.

3. Prepare the fruit according to the recipe directions — chop, crush, and so on.

4. Combine the fruit in a tall heavy saucepan with the sweetener and lemon juice according to the recipe directions.

5. Stir fruit over low heat until sugar dissolves. Then boil rapidly. As the mixture begins to thicken, stir frequently to prevent scorching.

6. Test for doneness. Use a candy, jelly, or deep-fat thermometer and boil until the temperature reaches 220°F or 8 degrees above the boiling point of water.

7. Remove from heat and skim off any foam that formed during boiling.

8. Pour into the sterilized jars, leaving ¼-inch headspace.

9. Wipe the rims of the jars with a clean, damp cloth.

10. Adjust the lids as the manufacturer recommends.

11. Place the filled jars on a rack in a preheated canner. Make sure the water covers the jars by at least 2 inches. Cover the canner and bring the water to a boil. Process for 5 minutes once the water has returned to a boil.

12. When the processing time is up, carefully remove the jars from the canner, using a jar lifter.

13. Cool the jars for 24 hours. Check the seals. Any jars not sealed should be refrigerated immediately and used within 2 weeks.

14. Remove screw bands, wipe sealed jars, label, date, and store in a cool, dry, dark place.

TIP   *If you don't have a jelly thermometer, you can test for gelling the old-fashioned way:*

__Sheet test.__ Dip a cool metal spoon into the boiling fruit mixture and lift the spoon out of the steam so the syrup runs off the side. When the mixture first starts to boil, the drops will be light and syrupy. As the syrup continues to boil, the drops will become heavier and will drop off the spoon two at a time. When the jellying point has been reached, the two drops form together and "sheet" off the spoon.

__Freezer test.__ Pour a small amount of the boiling mixture on a plate and put it in the freezer for a few minutes. If the mixture gels, it is done. During this test, the rest of the recipe should be removed from the heat.

Step-by-Step Jam- and Preserve-Making (With Added Pectin)

Note that these are general directions only. Follow the exact recipes that come in the package with the commercial pectin.

1. Preheat the canner, sterilize jars, and prepare lids according to the manufacturer's recommendations.

To preheat a boiling water bath canner, fill the boiling water bath canner with 4 to 4½ inches of hot tap water. To sterilize jars, set the jars on a rack inside the canner, bottom sides up. Turn the heat on high and bring to a boil. Boil for 10 minutes. Turn off the heat but leave the jars in the water until needed.

Wash and rinse all canning lids and screw bands. Treat the lids as directed by the manufacturer. Remember that lids can be used only once.

2. Wash your fruit thoroughly.

3. Prepare the fruit according to the recipe directions — chop, crush, and so on.

4. Measure the sugar and set aside.

5. Combine the fruit and lemon juice in a tall heavy saucepan. Add the pectin. Bring mixture to a full rolling boil that cannot be stirred down. Quickly add the sugar and return to a full rolling boil. Boil for 1 minute, stirring constantly.

6. Remove from heat and skim off any foam that formed during boiling.

7. Pour into the sterilized jars, leaving ¼-inch headspace.

8. Wipe the rims of the jars with a clean, damp cloth.

9. Adjust the lids as the manufacturer recommends.

10. Place the filled jars on a rack in a preheated canner. Make sure the water covers the jars by at least 2 inches. Cover the canner and bring the water to a boil. Process for 5 minutes once the water has returned to a boil.

11. When the processing time is up, carefully remove the jars from the canner, using a jar lifter.

12. Cool the jars for 24 hours. Check the seals. Any jars not sealed should be refrigerated immediately and used within 2 weeks.

13. Remove screw bands, wipe sealed jars, label, date, and store in a cool, dry, dark place.

Step-by-Step Jelly-Making (With Added Pectin)

Note that these are general directions only. Follow the exact recipes that come in the package with the commercial pectin. If you have already canned or frozen unsweetened fruit juice, you may use the juice and skip steps 1 to 4.

1. Wash fruit. Do not remove skins or cores. Place fruit in heavy-bot-tomed saucepan. To hard fruits, such as apples, add 1 cup of water per pound of fruit. For berries and grapes, use only enough water to prevent scorching. Crush soft fruits to start the flow of juice.

2. Bring to a boil over high heat. Stir frequently to prevent scorching. Reduce heat and simmer. Cook berries and grapes 10 minutes or less, until soft. Cook apples and other hard fruits for 20 to 25 minutes, until soft. Do not overcook.

3. Pour into a damp jelly bag or colander lined with a double thickness of damp cheesecloth and allow the juice to filter out.

4. Allow the juice to sit overnight so that any sediment can settle to the bottom. Do not squeeze fruit pulp, as the resulting juice will not be clear.

5. When you are ready to make the jelly, preheat the canner, sterilize jars, and prepare lids according to the manufacturer's recommendations.

To preheat a boiling water bath canner, fill the boiling water bath canner with 4 to 4½ inches of hot tap water. To sterilize jars, set the jars on a rack inside the canner, bottom sides up. Turn the heat on high and bring to a boil. Boil for 10 minutes. Turn off the heat but leave the jars in the water until needed.

Wash and rinse all canning lids and screw bands. Treat the lids as directed by the manufacturer. Remember that lids can be used only once.

6. Measure the sugar and set aside.

7. Measure the juice and mix with the pectin in a tall heavy saucepan. Bring mixture to a boil. Quickly add the sugar and return to a full rolling boil. Boil for 1 minute, stirring constantly.

8. Remove from heat and skim off any foam that formed during boiling.

9. Pour into the sterilized jars, leaving ¼-inch headspace.

10. Wipe the rims of the jars with a clean, damp cloth.

11. Adjust the lids as the manufacturer recommends.

12. Place the filled jars on a rack in a preheated canner. Make sure the water covers the jars by at least 2 inches. Cover the canner and bring the water to a boil. Process for 5 minutes once the water has returned to a boil.

13. When the processing time is up, carefully remove the jars from the canner, using a jar lifter.

14. Cool the jars for 24 hours. Check the seals. Any jars not sealed should be refrigerated immediately and used within 2 weeks.

15. Remove screw bands, wipe sealed jars, label, date, and store in a cool, dry, dark place.

Step-by-Step Jelly-Making (Without Added Pectin)

1. To ensure sufficient pectin for jelling, use 1 part (¼) slightly under-ripe fruit and 3 parts (¾) just-ripe fruit. Wash fruit. Do not remove skins

or cores. Place fruit in heavy-bottomed saucepan. To hard fruits, such as apples, add 1 cup of water per pound of fruit. For berries and grapes, use only enough water to prevent scorching. Crush soft fruits to start the flow of juice.

2. Bring to a boil over high heat. Stir frequently to prevent scorching. Reduce heat and simmer. Cook berries and grapes 10 minutes or less, until soft. Cook apples and other hard fruits for 20 to 25 minutes, until soft. Do not overcook.

3. Pour into a damp jelly bag or colander lined with a double thickness of damp cheesecloth and allow the juice to filter out.

4. Allow the juice to sit overnight so that any sediment can settle to the bottom. Do not squeeze fruit pulp as the resulting juice will not be clear.

5. When you are ready to make the jelly, preheat the canner, sterilize jars, and prepare lids according to the manufacturer's recommendations.

To preheat a boiling water bath canner, fill the boiling water bath canner with 4 to 4½ inches of hot tap water. To sterilize jars, set the jars on a rack inside the canner, bottom sides up. Turn the heat on high and bring to a boil. Boil for 10 minutes. Turn off the heat but leave the jars in the water until needed.

Wash and rinse all canning lids and screw bands. Treat the lids as directed by the manufacturer. Remember that lids can be used only once.

6. Combine up to 4 cups of fruit juice with sugar in a tall, heavy-bottomed saucepan, allowing ¾ cup sugar for each 1 cup of juice. Add 1 tablespoon lemon juice for each cup of fruit juice.

7. Stir to dissolve the sugar. Bring rapidly to a boil. Continue boiling until jelly reaches 220°F on a jelly thermometer or sheets off the spoon (see page 142).

8. Remove from heat and skim off any foam that formed during boiling.

9. Pour into the sterilized jars, leaving ¼-inch headspace.

10. Wipe the rims of the jars with a clean, damp cloth.

11. Adjust the lids as the manufacturer recommends.

12. Place the filled jars on a rack in a preheated canner. Make sure the water covers the jars by at least 2 inches. Cover the canner and bring the water to a boil. Process for 5 minutes once the water has returned to a boil.

13. When the processing time is up, carefully remove the jars from the canner, using a jar lifter.

14. Cool the jars for 24 hours. Check the seals. Any jars not sealed should be refrigerated immediately and used within 2 weeks.

15. Remove screw bands, wipe sealed jars, label, date, and store in a cool, dry, dark place.

Recipes

Here are some basic recipes to get you started with preserves. These are all recipes that do not use commercial pectin. If you are in a rush, make your preserves with commercial pectin, following the recipes that are included in the package, and cut the cooking time to about 10 minutes, compared to 30 to 50 minutes for the majority of the jam recipes.

∿ *Basic Berry Jam* ∿

7 to 8 half-pint jars

This recipe can be used with blackberries, blueberries, boysenberries, dewberries, gooseberries, loganberries, raspberries, and youngberries.

9 cups crushed berries
6 cups sugar

1. Preheat the canner, sterilize jars, and prepare lids while preparing the recipe.
2. Wash berries carefully.
3. Combine the berries and sugar in a tall heavy saucepan.
4. Bring slowly to a boil, stirring occasionally, until sugar dissolves. Then boil rapidly until thick, about 40 minutes. As the mixture begins to thicken, stir frequently to prevent scorching.
5. Test for doneness — 220°F on a thermometer or when the jam sheets off the spoon (see page 144).
6. Remove from heat and skim off any foam that formed during boiling.
7. Pour into the sterilized jars, leaving ¼-inch headspace. Wipe the rims of the jars with a clean, damp cloth. Adjust the lids as the manufacturer recommends.
8. Place the filled jars on a rack in a preheated canner. Process for 5 minutes once the water has returned to a boil.
9. When the processing time is up, carefully remove the jars from the canner, using a jar lifter.
10. Cool sealed jars. Check seals. Remove screw bands. Label. Store.

～ *Basic Peach Jam* ～

7 to 8 half-pint jars

2   quarts peeled, crushed peaches
½   cup water
6   cups sugar

1. Preheat the canner, sterilize jars, and prepare lids while preparing the recipe.
2. Prepare peaches. To peel peaches, dip in boiling water for 30 seconds. Then cool in ice water. Slip off skins. Remove pits. Crush by hand or pulse in a food processor.
3. Combine the peaches and water in a tall heavy saucepan; cook for 10 minutes.
4. Add the sugar and bring slowly to a boil, stirring occasionally, until sugar dissolves. Then boil rapidly until thick, about 15 minutes. As the mixture begins to thicken, stir frequently to prevent scorching.
5. Test for doneness — 220°F on a thermometer or when the jam sheets off the spoon (see page 144).
6. Pour into the sterilized jars, leaving ¼-inch headspace. Wipe the rims of the jars with a clean, damp cloth. Adjust the lids as the manufacturer recommends.
7. Place the filled jars on a rack in a preheated canner. Process for 5 minutes once the water has returned to a boil.
8. When the processing time is up, carefully remove the jars from the canner using a jar lifter.
9. Cool sealed jars. Check seals. Remove screw bands. Label. Store.

~ *Basic Strawberry Jam* ~

7 to 8 half-pint jars

2   quarts crushed strawberries

6   cups sugar

1. Preheat the canner, sterilize jars, and prepare lids while preparing the recipe.
2. Wash berries carefully.
3. Combine the berries and sugar in a tall heavy saucepan.
4. Bring slowly to a boil, stirring occasionally, until sugar dissolves. Then boil rapidly until thick, about 40 minutes. As the mixture begins to thicken, stir frequently to prevent scorching.
5. Test for doneness — 220°F on a thermometer or when the jam sheets off the spoon (see page 144).
6. Remove from heat and skim off any foam that formed during boiling.
7. Pour into the sterilized jars, leaving ¼-inch headspace. Wipe the rims of the jars with a clean, damp cloth. Adjust the lids as the manufacturer recommends.
8. Place the filled jars on a rack in a preheated canner. Process for 5 minutes once the water has returned to a boil.
9. When the processing time is up, carefully remove the jars from the canner using a jar lifter.
10. Cool sealed jars. Check seals. Remove screw bands. Label. Store.

∿ *Basic Plum Jam* ∿

About 8 half-pint jars

2	quarts chopped tart plums (4 pounds)
6	cups sugar
1½	cups water
¼	cup lemon juice

1. Preheat the canner, sterilize jars, and prepare lids while preparing the recipe.
2. Wash plums. Remove pits and chop.
3. Combine the plums, sugar, water, and lemon juice in a tall heavy saucepan.
4. Bring slowly to a boil, stirring occasionally, until sugar dissolves. Then boil rapidly until thick, about 20 minutes. As the mixture begins to thicken, stir frequently to prevent scorching.
5. Test for doneness — 220°F on a thermometer or when the jam sheets off the spoon (see page 144).
6. Pour into the sterilized jars, leaving ¼-inch headspace. Wipe the rims of the jars with a clean, damp cloth. Adjust the lids as the manufacturer recommends.
7. Place the filled jars on a rack in a preheated canner. Process for 5 minutes once the water has returned to a boil.
8. When the processing time is up, carefully remove the jars from the canner using a jar lifter.
9. Cool sealed jars. Check seals. Remove screw bands. Label. Store.

∼ *Basic Strawberry Preserves* ∼

About 4 half-pint jars

1½ quarts firm, ripe strawberries
5   cups sugar
⅓   cup lemon juice

1. Wash the strawberries. Hull and remove stems. Combine strawberries and sugar in a tall heavy-bottomed saucepan; let stand for 3 to 4 hours.
2. Bring the strawberries and sugar slowly to a boil, stirring occasionally, until sugar dissolves. Add lemon juice. Boil rapidly until the berries are soft and the syrup is clear, about 10 to 12 minutes.
3. Pour into a shallow pan. Let stand, uncovered, for 12 to 24 hours in a cool place. Shake pan occasionally to distribute berries through syrup.
4. Preheat the canner, sterilize jars, and prepare lids.
5. Heat preserves until boiling. Pour hot preserves into the sterilized jars, leaving ¼-inch headspace. Wipe the rims of the jars with a clean, damp cloth. Adjust the lids as the manufacturer recommends.
6. Place the filled jars on a rack in a preheated canner. Process for 5 minutes once the water has returned to a boil.
7. When the processing time is up, carefully remove the jars from the canner using a jar lifter.
8. Cool sealed jars. Check seals. Remove screw bands. Label. Store.

~ *Basic Apple Jelly* ~

4 to 5 half-pint jars

3 pounds apples
3 cups water
3 cups sugar
2 tablespoons lemon juice

1. Wash the apples. Chop into small pieces but do not peel or core. Combine with water in a heavy-bottomed saucepan and boil for about 25 minutes, or until apples are quite soft.
2. Pour into a damp jelly bag or colander lined with a double thickness of damp cheesecloth and allow the juice to filter out.
3. Allow the juice to sit overnight so that any sediment can settle to the bottom. Do not squeeze fruit pulp as the resulting juice will not be clear.
4. When you are ready to make the jelly, preheat the canner, sterilize jars, and prepare lids.
5. Combine 4 cups of apple juice with the sugar and lemon juice in a tall heavy-bottomed saucepan. Stir to dissolve the sugar.
6. Bring rapidly to a boil. Continue boiling until jelly reaches 220°F on a jelly thermometer or sheets off the spoon (see page 144).
7. Remove from heat and skim off any foam that formed during boiling.
8. Pour into the sterilized jars, leaving ¼-inch headspace. Wipe the rims of the jars with a clean, damp cloth. Adjust the lids as the manufacturer recommends.
9. Place the filled jars on a rack in a preheated canner and process for 5 minutes.
10. Cool sealed jars. Check seals. Remove screw bands. Label. Store.

∿ *Basic Grape Jelly* ∿

3 to 4 half-pint jars

3½ pounds grapes
½ cup water
3 cups sugar

1. Wash the grapes, remove stems. Crush grapes and combine with water in a heavy-bottomed saucepan. Bring to a boil, then reduce the heat and simmer for 10 minutes.
2. Pour into a damp jelly bag or colander lined with a double thickness of damp cheesecloth and allow the juice to filter out.
3. Allow the juice to sit overnight so that any sediment can settle to the bottom. Do not squeeze fruit pulp as the resulting juice will not be clear.
4. When you are ready to make the jelly, preheat the canner, sterilize jars, and prepare lids.
5. Combine 4 cups of grape juice with the sugar in a tall heavy-bottomed saucepan. Stir to dissolve the sugar.
6. Bring rapidly to a boil. Continue boiling until jelly reaches 220°F on a jelly thermometer or sheets off the spoon (see page 144).
7. Remove from heat and skim off any foam that formed during boiling.
8. Pour into the sterilized jars, leaving ¼-inch headspace. Wipe the rims of the jars with a clean, damp cloth. Adjust the lids as the manufacturer recommends.
9. Place the filled jars on a rack in a preheated canner and process for 5 minutes.
10. Cool sealed jars. Check seals. Remove screw bands. Label. Store.

TIP *Sometimes, despite your best efforts, a batch of jam, jelly, or preserves fails to gel. Don't call it a failure; call it a syrup and serve it on top of ice cream or pound cake.*

Fruits high in natural pectin

sour apples, sour blackberries, crabapples, cranberries,
currants, gooseberries, grapes (Eastern Concord), lemons,
loganberries, plums (not Italian), and quinces.

Fruits low in natural pectin

apricots, figs, grapes (Western Concord), guavas, peaches,
pears, plums (Italian), raspberries, and strawberries.
When making preserves with these fruits, plan to
use commercial pectin for best results.

TIP *You may remember seeing jelly jars sealed with paraffin. The USDA no longer recommends this. All jams and jellies must be processed in a boiling water bath to prevent mold.*

∽ *Orange Marmalade* ∽

About 7 half-pint jars

6   large oranges

2   medium-size lemons

6   cups water

About 6 cups sugar

1. Wash the fruit. Remove the peel from the oranges and thinly slice. Chop the orange pulp. You should have 4 cups of thinly sliced peel and 4 cups of orange pulp. Thinly slice the lemon. You should have 1 cup of slices.

2   Combine the fruit and water in a tall heavy-bottomed saucepan. Heat to simmer and simmer for 5 minutes. Cover and let stand for 12 to 18 hours.

3. Return the mixture to the stove and cook over medium heat until the peel is tender, about 1 hour.

4. Preheat the canner, sterilize jars, and prepare lids.

5. Measure fruit and liquid. For each 1 cup of fruit mixture, add 1 cup of sugar. Bring slowly to a boil, then cook rapidly until marmalade reaches 220°F or sheets off the spoon (see page 144), about 25 minutes.

6. Pour hot marmalade into the sterilized jars, leaving ¼-inch headspace. Wipe the rims of the jars with a clean, damp cloth. Adjust the lids as the manufacturer recommends.

7. Place the filled jars on a rack in a preheated canner. Process for 5 minutes once the water has returned to a boil.

8. When the processing time is up, carefully remove the jars from the canner using a jar lifter.

9. Cool sealed jars. Check seals. Remove screw bands. Label. Store.

⁓ *Oven-Baked Apple Butter* ⁓

5 to 6 half-pint jars

6   pounds apples (about 12 apples)
2   cups cider or water
　　Sugar, honey or maple syrup to taste
　　Cinnamon (optional)
　　Cloves (optional)

1. Wash the apples and cut into small pieces, leaving skins and cores. Combine with the cider or water in a large heavy saucepan. Bring to a boil and boil until apples are soft, about 30 minutes.
2. Puree apples in a hand-cranked strainer or food mill.
3. Place mixture in shallow baking dish and bake, uncovered, in a 200°F oven until quite thick, 6 to 8 hours. Stir occasionally.
4. One hour before cooking time is up, preheat the canner, sterilize jars, and prepare lids.
5. Sweeten apple butter to taste. Add a little cinnamon and cloves, if desired.
6. Pour into the sterilized jars, leaving ¼-inch headspace. Wipe the rims of the jars with a clean, damp cloth. Adjust the lids as the manufacturer recommends.
7. Place the filled jars on a rack in a preheated canner. Process for 5 minutes once the water has returned to a boil.
8. When the processing time is up, carefully remove the jars from the canner using a jar lifter.
9. Cool sealed jars. Check seals. Remove screw bands. Label. Store.

TIP *Although apple butter is most common, you can use the basic apple butter recipe to make delicious butters with grapes, peaches, pears, and plums.*

CHAPTER

9

What Went Wrong?
(And Other Commonly Asked Questions)

IT'S VERY DISCOURAGING to have anything go wrong when you are preserving food. Following directions carefully is the best way to avoid failures, but many factors can lead to a failure. The following commonly asked questions should help to solve — and prevent — many of your problems.

Freezing Questions

Should all vegetables be blanched before freezing?

In the past, it was thought that all vegetables, except onions and peppers, should be blanched before freezing. However, we have discovered that some vegetables are best unblanched. These are beans, young broccoli, chopped peppers, and sliced summer squash. Corn in husks, whole tomatoes, and chopped onions also can be frozen unblanched.

My frozen green beans are slimy and tough. How can I overcome that?

Green beans should not come in contact with water any more than necessary. Best results are obtained by freezing green beans that are unblanched or have been blanched in boilable bags for 6 to 8 minutes. They should be cooked by steaming or frying.

When do you start counting time when you blanch vegetables?

When blanching in boiling water (immersion blanching), timing is started as soon as water returns to a boil. If it takes longer than 2 minutes for the water to boil, you have blanched too much at once. Reduce the amount of vegetables in the next batch. Steam-blanch timing starts as soon as the cover is placed on the pan. Microwave-blanching begins when you press the start button.

What is the best way to freeze Sugar Snap peas?

Sugar Snap peas should be steam-blanched for 3 minutes and tray-frozen. Stir-fry Sugar Snaps for best cooked flavor.

Is it safe to freeze fruit without sugar?

Yes. Sugar does not function as a preservative when freezing, but it does help to maintain color and texture.

Can I use artificial sweeteners in place of sugar for freezing fruit?

Yes, since sugar isn't used as a preservative in frozen food. However, artificial sweeteners do not help the fruit maintain taste and texture as sugar does. To use artificial sweeteners, follow the directions on the package.

Why is my fruit sometimes mushy when thawed?

If fruits are frozen slowly, large ice crystals form and rupture cell walls, causing mushy fruit. For best results, freeze quickly and serve just as ice crystals are disappearing.

Drying Questions

Why did my dried food become moldy?

There are several possible reasons, all related to moisture. Perhaps the food was incompletely dried, or the container was not airtight, or the food was dried at too high a temperature, allowing the outside to harden before the inside moisture could escape. Prevent this in the future by testing the food within 1 week of drying. If there are signs of moisture in the food or in the jar, redry the food at 140°F until dry.

How can I prevent my fruit from sticking to the drying trays?

Spray trays with vegetable cooking spray. Also, gently lift food with a spatula after 1 hour of drying.

Why are there brown spots on my dried vegetables?

The temperature in your oven or dehydrator was too high.

Canning Questions

Sometimes my canning jars do not seal. Why?

Jars that come with mayonnaise, peanut butter, or commercially packed pickles may not fit the canning lids properly. Other reasons for unsealed jars are dented or rusty screw bands; nicked or cracked jars; handling lids with greasy fingers; not screwing bands on tightly enough; food, seeds, or herbs caught between the jar and the lid when sealing or when liquid is lost from the jars during the processing; or insufficient heat during processing.

What causes jars to crack in the canner?

Jars will crack if they are overfilled. Using a metal instrument or table knife to expel air will weaken the bottom of jars causing them to fall off during processing.

Must glass jars be sterilized by boiling before canning?

If the jars are to be processed for 10 minutes or more — as for most fruits and tomatoes — then sterilizing is not necessary. But be sure jars and lids are clean, and prepared according to manufacturer's directions before sealing jars. Sterilizing is necessary for most jams and jellies.

Why is liquid lost from jars during processing?

Loss of liquid may be due to packing jars too full. Failure to release air bubbles before sealing the jar will force out liquid when it begins to boil.

Should lost liquid be replaced?

No. Never open a jar and refill with liquid; this would let in bacteria and you would need to process again. Loss of liquid does not cause the food to spoil, though the food above the liquid may darken.

How can I tell if my canned food is spoiled?

The signs of spoilage are bulging lids, broken seals, leaks, change in color, foaming, unusual softness or slipperiness, spurting liquid when the jar is open, mold, or bad smells. If any of these signs are noted, do not use the food. Discard it where animals and humans cannot find it.

What makes canned food change color?

Darkening of food at the tops of jars may be caused by oxidation due to air in the jars or by too little heating or processing to destroy enzymes. Overprocessing may cause discoloration of foods throughout the containers. Iron and copper from cooking utensils or from water in some localities may cause brown, black, and gray colors in some foods. When canned corn turns brown, the discoloring may be due to the variety of corn, to the stage of ripeness, to overprocessing, or to copper or iron pans.

Is it safe to eat discolored foods?

The color changes noted above do not mean the food is unsafe to eat. However, spoilage may also cause color changes. Any canned food that has an unusual color should be examined carefully before use.

Is it safe to use home-canned food if the liquid is cloudy?

Cloudy liquid may be a sign of spoilage. But it may be caused by the minerals in hard water, or by starch from overripe vegetables. If liquid is cloudy, boil the food for 15 minutes before serving. Do not taste or use any food that foams during heating or has an off odor.

What causes an accumulation of black material on the underside of some lids?

Natural compounds in some foods cause deposits to form on the underside of lids. Unless the jar had been sealed and then become unsealed, this deposit is harmless. Do not use a jar of food that has become unsealed.

What causes a milky colored film on the outside of my jars?

Hard water leaves a mineral deposit on the outside of jars. To prevent this add ½ cup vinegar to each cannerful of water in hard water areas.

Is it safe to can food without salt?

Yes. Salt is used for flavor only and is not necessary for safe processing. Salt does help to retain the bright color of vegetables. If that is a concern of yours, you can add a small amount of ascorbic acid to the jars. (I use half of a 50-mg tablet.)

Is it all right to use preservatives in home canning?

No. Some canning powders or other chemical preservatives may be harmful.

Is processing time the same no matter what kind of stove you use?

As long as water in a boiling water bath canner remains boiling throughout the processing time, the processing times are the same.

Is it safe to can foods in the oven?

No. Oven canning is dangerous. Jars may explode. The temperature of the food in jars during oven-processing does not get high enough to insure destruction of spoilage bacteria in vegetables.

Why is open-kettle canning not recommended for fruits and vegetables?

In open-kettle canning, food is cooked in an ordinary kettle, then packed into hot jars and sealed without processing. For vegetables, the temperatures obtained in open-kettle canning are not high enough to destroy all the spoilage organisms that may be in the food. Spoilage bacteria may get in when the food is transferred from kettle to jar.

Is it safe to process sauces that contain low-acid foods in a boiling water bath canner?

If the proportion of low-acid foods to acid foods is very low it is safe. For example, ½ cup each of onion and green pepper to a 7-quart batch of spaghetti sauce would be safe. Dry herbs and onion and garlic powder are preferable to fresh herbs when canning by these methods. Process these sauces for the same length of time as the acid food.

Why do tomatoes sometimes float in the jar?

Tomatoes may float if they are overripe, if they are packed too loosely, or if they are overprocessed.

Is it safe to can overripe tomatoes in a boiling water bath?

Overripe tomatoes may be too low in acid to be safely canned by these methods. To be sure that the acid content is high enough (a pH rating below 4.5), add ¼ teaspoon of powdered citric acid per pint (½ teaspoon per quart), or 1 tablespoon lemon juice per pint (2 tablespoons per quart) before processing.

Why do the canning lids pop off when I can tomato juice that was liquefied in a blender?

Blenders incorporate a great deal of air into the vegetables they liquefy. The juice should be heated to boiling and simmered 5 minutes to exhaust that air before canning. Juice and purees from hand-cranked strainers should be handled the same way.

Why can't I use my microwave oven for making jam?

You can, but the results aren't guaranteed. When making microwave jams and jellies, it's important to use a recipe developed specifically for the microwave. It's even better to use a recipe developed for your particular microwave. Microwave jams and jellies boil over easily, so be sure to use a very deep bowl for cooking the product. You may not save any time in the process. Most recipes make such small quantities that canning is not necessary, since the resulting pint or half-pint can be stored in the refrigerator. For long-term storage, freezing or boiling water bath canning is necessary.

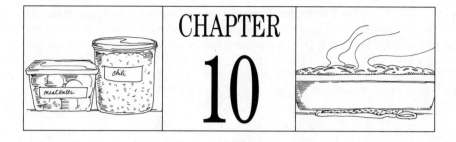

CHAPTER
10

Quick Harvest Meals

I HAVE TWO PIECES OF ADVICE for making harvest mealtimes easier: Incorporate the vegetables you are processing into your meals and have plenty of basic foods in the freezer, ready to be converted into instant meals.

Instant Meals

As winter slips into early spring, prepare extra meals to tuck away in the freezer for harvest dinners without hassle. You can freeze ahead dishes from recipes in this chapter, as well as individually frozen hamburg patties, beef and chicken stocks, and stew bases, crepes, pie crusts for quick meat pies or vegetables quiches, and favorite casseroles.

To save time in meal preparation, incorporate the vegetables you are working with into your meal plan for that day or the following day. For example, if you are canning or freezing spaghetti sauce, plan a spaghetti dinner. Remove from the freezer the number of servings of Freezer Meatballs (page 174) or frozen, cooked ground beef that you need, or brown some fresh beef. While the meat is heating in a pan of spaghetti sauce, prepare the pasta, and you have an almost instant dinner.

Diced Meats: The Basis of 13 Quick Meals

A supply of diced, cooked poultry, beef, pork, and ham frozen with their cooking broths can be the basis of a variety of different meals. Tender cuts can be roasted, cooled, diced, and packed with broth made from pan juices; less tender cuts should be simmered.

Roasts of beef, pork, ham, veal, chicken, and turkey up to 12 pounds can all be prepared by slow cooking in the oven — while you are busy elsewhere. To do so, prepare your roast as usual; do not stuff roasting chickens or turkeys. Early in the morning, roast the meat at the normal roasting temperature for 30 minutes. Reduce the oven temperature to 185°F (150°F for medium-rare roast beef and 200°F for a 10 to 12 pound turkey) and roast, uncovered, for 8 to 10 hours. The meat will be perfect for supper, and if you are a little late, it won't overcook.

Pot roast can be prepared the same way, adding vegetables if desired. Roast the meat covered for ½ hour at 375°F, reduce the temperature to 185°F, and roast 8 to 10 hours. Add seasonal vegetables, and you have a complete meal and enough leftovers to freeze for some instant meals.

Packages containing 2 cups of meat covered with broth will give you the greatest versatility. Here are just a few ideas for using these meats. I'm sure you will come up with more of your own.

- Combine with soup stock and seasonal vegetables for a hearty stew.
- Stir-fry with vegetables, add walnuts for variety.
- Make into hash.
- Cream chicken with new peas and carrots, and serve over hot biscuits.
- Make sandwiches, salads, quiches, and casseroles.
- Mix with homemade Indian relish, serve on hamburger rolls.
- Mix with homemade chutney, serve over rice or noodles.
- Add to cooked vegetables and stock, thicken with flour, and top with a crust or biscuits for a quick meat pie.
- Make chow mein.
- Mix with vegetables and eggs for a quick stove-top frittata.
- Mix with rice and vegetables for stir-fried rice.

Freeze-Ahead Recipes

The following recipes are for foods that can be prepared in advance to save meal preparation time during the busy harvest season. Serve part the day you make it and freeze the rest. Most are basic recipes that later can be used to create a variety of nourishing and delicious dishes using the sauces and vegetables you are preserving.

To save preparation time and energy, defrost frozen foods in the refrigerator overnight unless otherwise specified.

Preparation times given for all recipes in this chapter are based on the use of a food processor, blender, and electric mixer when preparing foods. If you do not use these appliances, be sure to add additional time. Also, when I added up the total work time, I did not include cooking, baking, and chilling times when I was free to perform other tasks.

∿ *3-in-1 Chicken Recipe* ∿

24 servings
2¼ hours (plus time for the chicken to cool and freeze)

12	pounds chicken fryer parts
1	tablespoon salt
1	large onion, cut in chunks
3	cups unbleached flour
3	cups crushed cornflakes
1¼	teaspoons baking powder
5	teaspoons salt
1	tablespoon garlic powder
1½	teaspoons dried tarragon leaves
1½	teaspoons dried chives
1½	teaspoons parsley flakes
3	eggs
¾	cup cold milk
2	teaspoons onion powder
	peanut oil for frying

1. Place the chicken in a large kettle with the salt and onion and water to cover. Bring to a boil, and simmer for 20 minutes.
2. Turn off the heat, and cool the chicken in the cooking broth (about 3 hours).
3. Drain well and save the stock for soup.
4. While the chicken is cooling, mix the flour, cornflake crumbs, baking powder, and seasonings. Set aside. Blend the eggs, milk, and onion powder. Set aside.
5. In a large, heavy skillet or electric frying pan, heat 2 inches of oil to 380°F. Dip the chicken pieces in the egg mixture and then in the

flour mixture. Fry until tender and golden brown on all sides. Remove the chicken from the frying pan, and drain on paper towels. It takes about 1½ hours to fry 12 pounds of chicken.

6. Cool completely (about 1 hour).
7. Tray-freeze for 12 hours.
8. When the chicken is frozen solid, package in large freezer bags to be used as needed.

Fried Chicken

Place frozen chicken parts on a well-greased baking sheet, and heat uncovered in a preheated, 400°F oven for 30 to 45 minutes. (Time depends on thickness of the chicken parts.)

Polynesian Chicken

While 8 pieces of chicken are heating in the oven as directed above, sauté 1 to 2 cups of vegetables (carrots, broccoli, onions, peppers) in 1 tablespoon of cooking oil until tender. Add 2 cups of homemade chutney (page 129) and heat through. Remove the cooked chicken from the oven, and top with the vegetable-chutney sauce. Return to the oven and bake an additional 10 to 12 minutes. Serves 4 with rice.

Barbecued Chicken

While 8 pieces of chicken are baking as in the directions given with the Fried Chicken, sauté 1 medium diced onion in 1 tablespoon oil until tender. Add 1 cup homemade catsup, 1 teaspoon honey, 1 tablespoon prepared mustard, 1 teaspoon salt, 1½ tablespoons cider vinegar, ½ teaspoon Worcestershire sauce, and ¼ teaspoon hot pepper sauce. Simmer for 20 minutes. When the chicken is heated through, top with the barbecue sauce and return to the hot oven for an additional 10 to 12 minutes. Serves 4.

~ *Chili* ~

25 servings
3¼ hours

4	pounds lean ground beef
2	tablespoons salad oil
3	cups diced onion
3	cups diced green pepper
8	cups cooked, drained kidney beans
2	quarts canned tomatoes
1½	cups tomato paste
1	cup water
2	tablespoons chili powder
½	teaspoon cayenne powder
½	teaspoon paprika
3	large bay leaves, crushed finely

1. Brown the beef in oil until it loses its red color. Add the remaining ingredients.
2. Cook uncovered until thick, about 2 hours. Stir occasionally.
3. Cool for 1 hour, stirring often.
4. Package in meal-size portions in straight-sided containers. Leave a 1-inch head space. Label. Freeze.

Defrost the chili overnight in the refrigerator or run cold water over the container to remove the frozen chili, and reheat in the top of a double boiler.

Serve with diced raw onion and grated Parmesan cheese, or serve in taco shells topped with diced onion, lettuce, and shredded cheddar cheese.

∾ *Meat Loaf* ∾

2 large or 4 small loaves
15 minutes (plus baking and cooling time)

3	pounds ground beef
1	pound ground pork
4	eggs
2	large onions, cut in chunks
6	ounces of bread (about 6 slices) torn in small pieces
1½	cups milk
¾	teaspoon dry mustard
1	teaspoon garlic powder (optional)
1½	teaspoons thyme
4	teaspoons salt
½	teaspoon pepper

1. Preheat the oven to 325°F. Place the beef and pork in a large bowl. Place the rest of the ingredients in a blender or food processor. Blend until smooth. Pour this over the meat, and mix thoroughly. Divide into two 9"x5"x3" loaf pans, or four 9"x4"x2½" pans.
2. Bake for 1½ hours (in large pans) or 1 hour (in small pans).
3. Remove the loaves from the oven. Drain excess fat. Cool completely.
4. Remove the loaves from the baking pans and wrap for the freezer. Label. Freeze.

Defrost overnight in the refrigerator and serve cold, surrounded by fresh vegetables or in sandwiches. Or reheat in a 305°F oven for 20 to 30 minutes.

You can top meat loaf slices with spaghetti sauce, Sweet-and-Sour Sauce, or hot mashed potatoes covered with a slice of your favorite cheese. Slip the meat back into the oven until the cheese melts or the sauces are heated through.

～ *Quick and Easy Lasagna* ～

12 large servings
1½ hours (plus time to make the sauce and freezing time)

4 cups spaghetti sauce (p. 137 or use
your favorite recipe)
1 pound uncooked lasagna noodles
2 pounds cottage cheese
2 cups sour cream
1 pound mozzarella cheese, sliced thinly
1 cup grated Parmesan cheese
2 cups water

1. Preheat the oven to 350°F.
2. Foil line two 9"x13" casserole dishes. Spread 1 cup of spaghetti sauce in the bottom of each dish. In a bowl, mix the cottage cheese with the sour cream. Layer the ingredients in the casserole dishes, beginning with the noodles, followed by the cottage cheese and sour cream mixture, then the mozzarella, ½ cup sauce, and finally the Parmesan cheese. Repeat 1 more layer, dividing the ingredients evenly between the casserole dishes. Pour 1 cup water around the sides of each dish.
3. Cover tightly with foil and bake for 1 hour. If both casseroles are to be frozen, remove from oven after 1 hour. If a pan of lasagna is to be eaten, bake it uncovered an additional 15 minutes or until the noodles are tender. Let it stand 15 minutes before serving.
4. Cool for 2 hours.
5. Freeze.
6. Remove the casserole from the baking dish. Wrap with freezer wrap or foil. Return to the freezer.

Return to a baking dish and defrost in the refrigerator overnight. Bake covered in a preheated, 350°F oven for 30 to 40 minutes. Let the lasagna stand 15 minutes before serving.

∼ *Ratatouille* ∼

10 to 12 servings
45 minutes

Ratatouille is a great harvest dish. It makes good use of eggplant,
zucchini, and peppers. You can serve it hot or chilled, or freeze it for
enjoying later. In fact, making ratatouille is an excellent way
to preserve extra eggplant and zucchini. You can serve this as a
vegetarian main dish, or serve it as a topping for rice or pasta.
For nonvegetarians, stir in 2 to 3 cups of
chopped, cooked turkey or chicken.

6   tablespoons olive oil

3   onions, chopped

4   garlic cloves, minced

2   medium to large, peeled eggplants, diced

2   green peppers, diced

2   red peppers, diced

8   medium zucchini, sliced

6   tomatoes, chopped, or 1 (28-ounce) can whole
peeled tomatoes, drained and chopped

1   (6-ounce) can tomato paste

1   cup water

1   cup chopped fresh parsley

1   cup chopped fresh basil

Salt and pepper to taste

1. In a large Dutch oven, heat the oil. Add the onions, garlic, eggplant, and peppers and sauté until the vegetables are limp, about 8 minutes.
2. Stir in the zucchini, tomatoes, tomato paste, and water. Heat to boiling. Reduce heat to medium, cover, and cook for about 15 minutes.
3. Add herbs and salt and pepper to taste. Continue cooking, uncovered, for about 10 more minutes.
4. Cool for 1 hour, stirring often.

5. Package in meal-size portions in straight-sided containers. Leave 1-inch headspace. Label. Freeze.

For a quick supper on the day you make this, serve the Ratatouille over rice or pasta, topped with grated cheese, with a fresh garden salad on the side.

⁓ *Freezer Meatballs* ⁓

Approximately 100 meatballs
1½ hours

5	pounds lean ground beef
3	eggs
1½	cups quick-cooking oatmeal
¾	cup grated Parmesan cheese
3	large cloves garlic
2	large onions, coarsely chopped
1½	teaspoons dried oregano
2	tablespoons dried basil
2	teaspoons crushed red pepper
1	tablespoon salt
¾	teaspoon black pepper

1. Place the beef in a large bowl. Put the eggs, oatmeal, cheese, garlic, onions, herbs, and spices in a blender or food processor. Puree until smooth. Add to the beef and mix thoroughly with your hands.
2. Preheat the oven to 400°F.
3. Shape the meat mixture into 1-inch balls. Place on lightly greased cookie sheets.
4. Bake for 25 minutes at 400°F.
5. Cool at room temperature for 30 minutes. Drain fat.
6. Tray-freeze. When frozen, pack in large plastic freezer bags. Freeze.

For a quick 15-minute supper on the day you are making Jan's Spicy Spaghetti Sauce, ladle some sauce into a saucepan; add the desired number of frozen meatballs. Simmer until the meatballs are cooked through (about 15 minutes). Meanwhile, prepare some quick-cooking vermicelli (Mueller's has one that cooks in 5 minutes). Serve with fresh garden salad.

Another quick meal can be made by heating the meatballs in spaghetti sauce, and serving on hamburger rolls for hot meatball sandwiches.

∼ *Baked Beans* ∼

10 to 12 servings
45 minutes (plus overnight soaking and 4 hours baking)

2	pounds navy pea beans
4	quarts cold water
1½	cups brown sugar
2	teaspoons dry mustard
1	teaspoon salt
½	teaspoon pepper
½	teaspoon hot pepper sauce
¼	cup tomato paste
	Boiling water
12	small onions
12	slices fresh (uncured) bacon

1. Rinse the beans with cold water. Place in a 10-quart kettle. Add 4 quarts of cold water. Let stand overnight.
2. Cook the beans in the water they were soaked in. Cover the kettle; bring the beans to a boil. Then lower the heat and simmer until tender. Skim off the foam as it rises to the top.
3. Drain the beans. Preheat the oven to 325°F.
4. Line two 2-quart baking dishes with foil. Divide the beans between the two baking dishes. Put half of the dry mustard, salt, pepper, hot pepper sauce, and tomato paste in each dish. Cover the beans with boiling water. Stir well. Top with onions; then fresh bacon slices.
5. Bake, uncovered, for 4 hours, adding water as necessary.
6. Cool at room temperature for 1½ hours.
7. Freeze for 12 hours.
8. Remove the frozen beans from the baking dishes. Overwrap with freezer wrap or foil. Label and return the packages to the freezer.

Defrost frozen beans in the refrigerator. Place the foil package in a baking dish. Bake, uncovered, in a 325°F oven for 1 hour. Add a small amount of boiling water, if necessary. Or place the frozen casserole back into a casserole dish. Put in a 325°F oven and bake covered for 1 hour, uncover, and bake another hour. Add boiling water if necessary.

Cold baked beans can be mashed, with raw onion to taste, for a sandwich filling. This is delicious served on rye bread with a spicy mustard.

Harvest-Time Dishes

In the thick of preserving vegetables, you can save time by cooking a dinner based on the vegetable you are processing. Base the whole meal around the vegetable, or use a vegetable dish to supplement some of the casseroles and other goodies you have tucked away in the freezer for busy days.

Here are a few of my favorite vegetable recipes.

∼ Magic Crust Broccoli Pie ∼

4 to 6 servings
1 hour

2   cups chopped cooked broccoli
1   cup chopped cooked ham
¾   cup shredded cheddar cheese
½   cup unbleached flour
⅛   teaspoon salt
¾   teaspoon double-acting baking powder
1   tablespoon shortening
2   eggs
¾   cup milk

1. Preheat the oven to 350°F.
2. Layer the broccoli, ham, and cheese in a well-oiled 9-inch pie plate. Blend the remaining ingredients in a blender, food processor, or with an electric hand mixer. Pour over the cheese layer.
3. Bake, uncovered, for 40 minutes.
4. Let stand for 10 minutes before serving.

⌒ *Vegetable Platter with Peanut Sauce* ⌒

4 servings
1 hour

Vegetables:

4	large carrots (scrubbed and peeled, if desired)
4	medium potatoes, pared
½	medium head of cabbage, cut in wedges
2	cups whole green beans
1	medium-size bunch of broccoli, separated into slender stalks
1½	cups water

Sauce:

¾	cup peanut butter
4	tablespoons chopped peanuts
½	cup beef stock, bouillon, or water
½	cup coffee cream
1	tablespoon lemon juice
1	clove garlic, minced finely
¼	teaspoon crushed red pepper

1. Prepare the vegetables.
2. Bring the water to a boil in a large kettle. Add the carrots and potatoes. Reduce heat, and cook for 15 minutes.
3. Add the cabbage, beans, and broccoli. Continue cooking until the potatoes are tender and the other vegetables are tender crisp, about 15 minutes.
4. Drain the liquid, and keep the vegetables warm. Meanwhile, combine the sauce ingredients in medium-size saucepan, and cook over medium heat until heated through.
5. Arrange the vegetables on a large platter and top with the sauce.

∽ *Cheese Stuffed Peppers* ∽

4 servings
45 minutes

4 large green peppers, seed pods removed
1 large tomato, scalded, peeled, and cubed
2 teaspoons fresh basil, finely chopped,
   or ½ teaspoon dried
¼ teaspoon salt
   Dash pepper or cayenne
½ pound sharp cheddar cheese, cut in ¼-inch cubes
½ pound Swiss cheese, cut in ¼-inch cubes

1. Prepare the vegetables and boil water in a kettle. Preheat the oven to 375°F.
2. Place 2 inches of boiling water in a 4-quart kettle. Arrange the peppers in a standing position and parboil for 6–8 minutes.
3. Drain the peppers. Place them standing upright in a lightly greased baking dish. Combine the tomato and seasonings and spoon into the peppers, dividing the filling evenly. Mix the cheese together and stuff into the peppers, rounding off the tops.
4. Bake until the peppers are hot and the cheese is melted, about 20 minutes.

∼ *Spinach Surprise* ∼

6 to 8 servings
1 hour

1	cup unbleached flour
¾	teaspoon salt
1¼	teaspoons baking powder
2	tablespoons shortening, melted and cooled
¼	cup milk
4	eggs
¼	cup fresh parsley, finely chopped
½	cup diced onion
1½	cups cooked spinach, well drained
¼	cup grated Parmesan cheese
4	ounces Monterey Jack cheese, cut in ¼-inch cubes
1½	cups cottage cheese
½	teaspoon salt
2	cloves garlic, minced finely

1. Preheat the oven to 375°F.
2. Grease a 12"x7½"x2" baking dish.
3. Mix the flour, ¼ teaspoon of the salt, baking powder, shortening, milk, 2 of the eggs, parsley, and onion. Beat vigorously for 20 strokes. Spread the mixture in the baking dish. Combine the remaining ingredients, mix well, and spoon evenly over batter mixture.
4. Bake until set, approximately 30 minutes.
5. Let stand for 5 minutes before serving.

∿ *Harvest-Time Acorn Squash* ∿

4 servings
1¼ hours

2   medium acorn squash
Boiling water
3   tablespoons melted butter
¼   cup brown sugar, packed
¼   teaspoon cinnamon
¼   teaspoon salt
⅛   teaspoon nutmeg
1   cup prepared applesauce
2   teaspoons butter

1. Preheat the oven to 375°F. Begin boiling water in a kettle.
2. Wash the squash, cut in half lengthwise, remove seeds and stringy fibers. Place the squash, cut side down, on a rack in a shallow baking pan. Pour in ½ inch boiling water. Cover the pan with a tight-fitting lid or with tinfoil.
3. Bake for 30 minutes.
4. Remove the pan from the oven. Pour off the water, turn the squash cut side up. Combine the melted butter, 2 tablespoons of sugar, and the spices. Smooth over the edges of the squash pieces. Fill the centers with applesauce; top with the remaining brown sugar and butter.
5. Bake until the squash is tender, approximately 15 minutes.

～ *Cucumbers in Dill Sauce* ～

4 servings
35 minutes

4   slender 5-inch to 6-inch cucumbers
½   cup plain yogurt
½   cup sour cream
1   tablespoon chopped fresh dill or
    1 teaspoon dried dill seed
¼   cup chopped green onions

1. Peel the cucumbers and slice thinly.
2. Combine the remaining ingredients and pour over cucumbers. Mix well.
3. Cover and chill in the freezer for ½ hour.

～ *Pesto Pasta* ～

4 to 6 servings
25 minutes

For a more satisfying dish, add 1 to 2 cups of lightly steamed vegetables, such as broccoli, green beans, diced carrots, or a combination of vegetables, to the sauce.

3　tablespoons pine nuts, walnuts, or sunflower seeds

2　garlic cloves

½　cup herb paste (see page 107)

½–¾　cup grated Parmesan, Romano, or Asiago cheese

½–¾　cup high-quality olive or other salad oil

Salt and pepper to taste

1 pound pasta

1. Begin heating salted water for the pasta.
2. In a food processor or blender, grind the nuts. Add garlic and grind again. Add herb paste and cheese and process very briefly. With the motor running, slowly drizzle in the oil until the mixture has a sauce consistency. Season to taste with salt and pepper. Set aside.
3. Cook the pasta according to the package directions. Drain. Immediately toss the hot pasta with the pesto. Serve at once, passing additional grated cheese at the table.

∼ *Pasta with Garden Salad Sauce* ∼

4 servings
½ hour

This is delicious served with Herb-Fried Chicken.

2	large tomatoes, scalded, peeled, and chopped
1	medium green pepper, chopped coarsely
1½	cups coarsely chopped broccoli
1	cup coarsely chopped onion
1	large clove garlic, minced finely
3	quarts water
¼	cup salad oil
3	tablespoons cider vinegar
½	teaspoon dried basil or 2 tablespoons fresh basil, chopped finely
4	cups precooked pasta

1. Prepare the vegetables.
2. Put 3 quarts of water on to boil. Heat the salad oil in a large heavy skillet. Add all vegetables, *except the tomatoes*. Sauté the vegetables until tender crisp.
3. Add the tomatoes, vinegar, basil. Cook for 2 minutes. Keep warm.
4. Drop the pasta into the boiling water. Return the water to a boil. Turn off the heat and let the pasta remain in the water for 1 minute.
5. Drain the pasta. Top with vegetable sauce and serve.

～ *Squash Bisque* ～

6–8 servings
½ hour

1½	cups diced onion
1	cup diced celery
1	cup chopped mushrooms
3	tablespoons copped fresh parsley or 1 tablespoon dried
¼	cup chopped green pepper
¼	cup chopped sweet red pepper
2	cups mashed cooked winter squash
2	tablespoons butter
2	cups chicken stock, bouillon, or water
	Dash of cayenne pepper
1	cup milk
¼	cup light cream
	Salt and pepper to taste

1. Prepare the vegetables.

2. Melt the butter in a heavy 4-quart saucepan. Sauté the onion, celery, mushrooms, parsley, and green and red peppers until the onions are limp but not brown, about 5 minutes.

3. Add the squash, stock, cayenne pepper, and salt and pepper to taste. Simmer for 15 minutes.

4. Add the milk and cream, and reheat just to boiling.

～ *Dutch-Style Green Beans* ～

4 servings
15 minutes

3 slices bacon, diced
1 medium onion, diced
2 teaspoons cornstarch
¼ teaspoon salt
¼ teaspoon dry mustard
½ cup chicken broth or water
1 tablespoon cider vinegar
1 tablespoon brown sugar
2 cups chopped cooked green beans
1 hard-boiled egg, chopped

1. Sauté the bacon in a large skillet until crisp. Remove from the pan. Add the onion to the pan drippings and sauté until tender.
2. Blend in the cornstarch, salt, and mustard. Stir in the broth and cook, stirring constantly, until thickened.
3. Stir in the vinegar and sugar; add the beans and heat until bubbly. Serve with bacon and chopped egg.

∿ *Lettuce and Green Pea Soup* ∿

4 to 6 servings
40 minutes

2 cups fresh peas (frozen peas may be substituted)
8 cups shredded crisp head lettuce
½ cup sliced green onions
1 clove garlic, minced finely (optional)
2 cups chicken broth or bouillon
1 teaspoon sugar
1 teaspoon salt
½ teaspoon dried chervil
   Dash pepper
1½ cups light cream

1. Shell the peas and chop the vegetables in a food processor.
2. In a heavy 4-quart Dutch oven, combine the lettuce, peas, onions, garlic, and broth. Cover the kettle and bring the contents to a boil. Reduce the heat and simmer for 15 minutes.
3. Pour half of the mixture into a blender and puree until smooth. Pour into a bowl. Put the balance of lettuce mixture in the blender with the sugar, salt, chervil, and pepper. Puree until smooth.
4. Return all the lettuce mixture to a saucepan if you are going to serve it warm and mix well, or mix well in a bowl to serve cold. Add the cream. Reheat or chill. Serve.

∿ *15 Creamed Vegetable Soups* ∿

Each soup makes 4 servings

Many delicious, fresh summer soups can be made from vegetable purees. These soups can be served hot or cold, as appetizers or as the main meal. Either way they are quick and satisfying. They take just 10 to 15 minutes to make with prepared purees from fresh cooked, canned, or frozen cooked vegetables. On the chart on pages 188-189 you will find suggested ingredients and amounts for fifteen different creamed vegetable soups. In each case, to make the puree, combine 3 cups of cooked vegetables with 1 cup of stock or water and puree in the blender. Purees for soup are best made with chicken stock, but vegetarians may wish to use water and increase the seasonings for extra flavor.

1. Sauté the onion in butter until tender but not brown.
2. Place in the blender with half of the puree and half of the cream or milk. Blend until smooth. Pour into a saucepan (or bowl, if to be eaten chilled). Blend the remaining ingredients; add to first half. Stir well. To serve warm, reheat just until piping hot.
3. To serve cold, chill for several hours.

TIP *As with all soups, these are better if made ahead so that flavors can blend. All the soups can be garnished with chopped chives, parsley, croutons, bacon bits, yogurt, sour cream, or grated Parmesan cheese.*

～ *15 Creamed Vegetable Soups* ～

3 Cups Vegetable Puree	Onion	Butter
Beans, Green or Yellow	¼ cup	1 tablespoon
Beets	½ cup	1 tablespoon
Broccoli and Cauliflower	½ cup	2 tablespoons
Cabbage	¼ cup	1 tablespoon
Carrots	¼ cup	2 tablespoons
Corn	⅛ cup	2 tablespoons
Cucumbers	½ cup	2 tablespoons
Greens	¼ cup	2 tablespoons
Onions		2 tablespoons
Peas, Green or Sugar Snap	½ cup	2 tablespoons
Summer Squash	1 cup	2 tablespoons
Tomatoes	½ cup	2 tablespoons
Winter Squash I	¼ cup	2 tablespoons
Winter Squash II		2 tablespoons

Light Cream or Milk	Seasonings
1 cup	2 dashes Tabasco, ¼ teaspoon garlic powder, ½ teaspoon basil, salt and pepper to taste
	¼ teaspoon garlic powder, 1 cup stock, 1 tablespoon lemon juice, ½ teaspoon celery salt, salt and pepper to taste, top with yogurt or sour cream
1 cup	4 ounces cheddar cheese, salt and pepper to taste
1 cup	½ teaspoon celery salt, salt and pepper to taste
1 cup	¼ teaspoon curry powder, salt and pepper to taste
1 cup	1 cup diced chicken, 1 tablespoon chopped chives, salt and pepper to taste
1 cup	salt and pepper to taste, top with yogurt or sour cream
1 cup	½ teaspoon cayenne, salt and pepper to taste, top with yogurt or sour cream
1 cup	4 ounces cheddar cheese, 1 tablespoon cooking sherry, salt and pepper to taste
1 cup	½ teaspoon tarragon, salt and pepper to taste
1 cup	½ teaspoon curry powder, salt and pepper to taste
1 cup	6 ounces American cheese, salt and pepper to taste
1 cup	½ teaspoon cayenne, salt and pepper to taste
	2 tablespoons brown sugar, ½ teaspoon allspice, ½ cup applesauce

8 Freeze-Ahead Ideas

Cheese. Grate cheese for casseroles, pizza, and toppings and store in your freezer.

Toppings. Prepare bread and cracker crumbs for toppings and coatings and store in your freezer.

Turkey. Cook a large turkey with dressing. Slice the meat and cover with dressing and gravy. Freeze in meal-size portions.

Individual servings. Fix favorite foods or leftovers in individual foil or boilable-bag servings. Always chill any foods that have been pre-cooked before packaging. Refrigerate for use within a day or so, or freeze for longer storage. Hurry-up meals can be prepared by just popping foil packages in the oven or boilable bags in a pan of hot water. There is little or no clean-up after.

Quick breakfasts. Make extra pancakes and waffles and tuck some away in the freezer to give you a few extra minutes on summer mornings to package tray-frozen foods. The kids can fix their own breakfast by warming the waffles and pancakes in the toaster and topping them with fresh fruit, preserves, and a little yogurt.

Ground beef. Cook several pounds of ground beef; divide it into several containers to be tossed quickly into sauces and quick casserole dishes that require cooked ground beef.

Quick desserts. If your family loves desserts, spring is the best time to freeze a few extra fruit breads, whole grain and fruit bars, cookies, and sheet cakes for busier times. Bake sheet cakes and divide in 4. Do not frost. These can be used later as single-layer cakes, double-layer birthday cakes (2 sections), or served with fresh fruit and toppings.

Tray-freeze meats. Meatballs, meat patties, fried chicken, and similar foods can be tray-frozen and packed in plastic bags. At mealtimes, take out the number of servings needed.

8 More Harvest-Time Meal-Planning Tips

Layered salad. Layer up a make-ahead salad in a large bowl. Layer shredded lettuce, peas, green onions, cooked macaroni, chopped tomatoes, sliced cucumbers, chopped walnuts, and diced chicken. Make a creamy dressing of 1½ cups mayonnaise, ¼ cup light cream, and 2 tablespoons chopped chives. Pour the dressing over the salad but do not toss. Cover with foil or plastic wrap and chill for several hours or overnight.

Slow cookers. Slow-cooked meals are time- and energy-savers. To adapt your own favorite stew recipe to the slow cooker, triple the recommended cooking time for the low setting or double it for the high setting. When cooking vegetables in the slow cooker, parboil them 6 to 10 minutes before adding to the pot. Always place vegetables in the bottom of the slow cooker with the meat on the top. Reduce the amount of liquid in your stew or casserole by about ⅓ and reduce the seasoning by at least that much.

Quick fillers. Precook several servings of potatoes, rice, pasta, and hard-boiled eggs when you have an extra hour or so one day a week. They can be used for quick dishes during the week, such as potato salad, hash-browned potatoes, corned beef hash, creamed potatoes, soups, stir-fried rice, spaghetti, and egg salad.

Pasta and rice. Undercook pasta and rice by 4 to 5 minutes for baked dishes and 2 to 3 minutes for meals not requiring additional baking time. To reheat pasta for use with a quick sauce, bring lightly salted water to a boil, add pasta and return to a boil, drain, and add sauce. To reheat rice, place in a fine mesh sieve over boiling water, keep water simmering until rice is heated through, fluffing with a fork once or twice while heating; this just takes a few minutes.

Quick main meals. Cook a large roast, meat loaf, turkey, pan of lasagna, or stew on the Friday evening of a harvest weekend. It will serve as a quick main meal with the addition of a fresh salad, bread, and beverage — even if company drops in. Leftover meats and meat loaf can be used for sandwiches.

Ready-cut vegetables. Dice onions, celery, green peppers, and carrots. Place in plastic bags and refrigerate. This saves time when preparing soups, salads, and casseroles. If all the vegetables are not used up in 4 to 5 days, freeze the remainder. These will not be good for fresh salads after they are frozen, but can be used in all other ways including in stir-fried dishes and fried rice.

Salad makings. Tear salad greens (cut greens will turn brown around the edges when stored), wash, and spin dry; place them in plastic bags. They will maintain the crispness up to a week. To keep tomatoes firm when sliced ahead, slice them vertically and store in a separate bag.

Frozen casseroles. Line casserole dishes with foil when making casseroles to be frozen. After the casseroles are frozen, they can be removed from the baking dish, freeing it for another use.

Appendix

Handy Reference Charts

Approximate Yield of Fruits from Fresh

Fruit	Fresh	Frozen Pints	Canned Quarts
Applesauce	1¼–1½ lb.	1	
Berries	1 crate (24 qt.)	32–36	12–18
	1⅓–1½ pt.	1	
Cantaloupes	1 dozen (28 lb.)	22	
	1–1¼ lb.	1	
Cherries, Sweet or Sour	1 bu. (56 lb.)	36–44	22–32
	1¼–1½ lb.	1	
Cranberries	1 box (25 lb.)	50	
	½ lb.	1	
Currants	22 qt. (3 lb.)	4	
	¾ lb.	1	
Peaches	1 bu. (48 lb.)	32–48	18–24
	1–1½ lb.	1	
Pears	1 bu. (50 lb.)	40–50	20–25
	1–1½ lb.	1	
Plums and Prunes	1 bu. (56 lb.)	38–56	24–30
	1–1½ lb.	1	
Raspberries	1 crate (24 pt.)	24	12–18
	1 pt.	1	
Rhubarb	15 lb.	15–22	
	⅔–1 lb.	1	
Strawberries	1 crate (24 qt.)	38	
	⅔ qt.	1	

Approximate Yield of Vegetables from Fresh

Vegetable	Fresh	Frozen Pints	Canned Quarts
Asparagus	1 crate (12 2-lb. bunches)	15–22	
	1–1½ lb.	1	
Beans, Lima (in pods)	1 bu. (32 lb.)	12–16	6–10
	2–2½ lb.	1	
Beans, Snap, Green, & Wax	1 bu. (30 lb.)	30–45	12–20
	⅔–1 lb.	1	
Beet Greens	15 lb.	10–15	3–8
	1–1½ lb.	1	
Beets (without tops)	1 bu. (52 lb.)	35–42	15–24
	1¼–1½ lb.	1	
Broccoli	1 crate (25 lb.)	24	
	1 lb.	1	
Carrots (without tops)	1 bu. (50 lb.)	32–40	16–25
	1¼–1½ lb.	1	
Cauliflower	2 medium heads	3	
	1⅓ lb.	1	
Chard	1 bu. (12 lb.)	8–12	3–8
	1–1½ lb.	1	
Collard Greens	1 bu. (12 lb.)	8–12	3–8
	1–1½ lb.	1	
Corn, Sweet	1 bu. (35 lb.) (in husks)	14–17 (whole kernel)	6–10 (whole kernel)
	2–2½ lb.	1	
Kale	1 bu. (18 lb.)	12–18	3–8
	1–1½ lb.	1	
Mustard Greens	1 bu. (12 lb.)	8–12	3–8
	1–1½ lb.	1	

Vegetable	Fresh	Frozen Pints	Canned Quarts
Peas (in pods)	1 bu. (30 lb.)	12–15	5–10
	2–2½ lb.	1	
Peppers, Sweet	⅔ lb. (3 peppers)	1	
Pumpkins	3 lb.	2	1
Spinach	1 bu. (18 lb.)	12–18	3–8
	1–1½ lb.	1	
Squash, Summer	1 bu. (40 lb.)	32–40	10–20
	1–1¼ lb.	1	
Squash, Winter	3 lb.	2	

Timetable for Blanching Vegetables
for the Freezer

Vegetable	Blanch in Boilable Bag, 4 Bags at a Time (in minutes)	Blanch by Immersion or Steam, 1 Pound at a Time (in minutes)	Suitable for Freezing Unblanched
Beans, Green & Wax	6–8	3–4	Yes
Beets			No
Broccoli		5	Yes
Cabbage			Yes
Carrots	8–10	3–4	No
Corn on the Cob	10	6–8	Yes
Corn, Whole Kernel	6		No
Greens	Stir-fry until wilted: 2–3 minutes		No
Peas, Green	4	2	No
Summer Squash	5		Yes

Drying Herbs in a Dehydrator

(Set dehydrator at 110°F.)

HERB	DEHYDRATOR DRYING TIME
Anise	10–12 hours
Basil	8–12 hours
Cilantro	6–8 hours
Dill, leaves	6–8 hours
Dill seeds	4–6 hours
Fennel, leaves	6–8 hours
Fennel seeds	4–8 hours
Garlic, chopped	6–8 hours
Marjoram	6–8 hours
Mint	6–8 hours
Oregano	4–8 hours
Parsley	6–8 hours
Rosemary	6–8 hours
Sage	8–12 hours
Savory	6–8 hours
Tarragon	6–8 hours
Thyme	6–8 hours

Timetable for Microwave Blanching
Vegetables for the Freezer

Vegetable	Amount Vegetable	Amount Water	Microwave Blanch on High (100% power)
Asparagus	2 cups (1 pound)	¼ cup	3 minutes
Beans, Green and Wax	3 cups (1 pound)	½ cup	4 minutes
Broccoli	3 cups (1½ pounds)	½ cup	5 minutes
Carrots	4 cups (1¼ pounds)	½ cup	3½ minutes
Cauliflower	1 head, cut in florets (1 pound)	½ cup	4½ minutes
Corn on the Cob	4 ears	¼ cup	3 minutes
Corn, Whole Kernel	2 cups	⅛ cup	3 to 3½ minutes
Greens	12 cups (1 pound)	⅛ cup	3½ minutes
Peas	2 cups (2 pounds)	¼ cup	2 minutes
Sugar Snap Peas, Snow Peas	2 cups (1 pound)	⅛ cup	2½ to 4
Summer Squash	1 pound	¼ cup	

Procedure: Prepare the vegetable, chopping into even-size pieces. Arrange in microwave-safe container. Add water. Cover. Stir or rearrange halfway through blanching time. Chill, pack, freeze.

Boiling Water Bath Processing Times at Altitudes Over 1,000 Feet

Boiling Water Bath Canner

FRUIT OR VEGETABLE	STYLE OF PACK	JAR SIZE	PROCESS TIME IN MINUTES		
			1,000 TO 3,000 FT	3,001 TO 6,000 FT	OVER 6,000
Apple Juice	Hot	Pt or Qt	10	10	15
Apples	Hot	Pt or Qt	25	30	35
Applesauce	Hot	Pt	20	20	25
		Qt	25	30	35
Apricots	Hot	Pt	25	30	35
		Qt	30	35	40
	Raw	Pt	30	35	40
		Qt	35	40	45
Cherries	Hot	Pt	20	20	25
		Qt	25	30	35
	Raw	Pt or Qt	30	35	40
Cranberry Sauce	Hot	Pt or Qt	20	20	25
Grape Juice	Hot	Pt or Qt	10	10	15
Nectarines	Hot	Pt	25	30	35
		Qt	30	35	40
	Raw	Pt	30	35	40
		Qt	35	40	45
Peaches	Hot	Pt	25	30	35
		Qt	30	35	40
	Raw	Pt	30	35	40
		Qt	35	40	45
Pears	Hot	Pt	25	30	35
		Qt	30	35	40
Plums	Raw or Hot	Pt	25	30	35
		Qt	30	35	40
Rhubarb	Hot	Pt or Qt	20	20	25
Tomato Puree	Hot	Pt	40	45	50
		Qt	50	55	60
Tomatoes, Whole	Raw	Pt	45	50	55
		Qt	50	55	60

Note: To adjust processing times for jellied fruit products, add 1 minute to processing time for each 1,000 feet of altitude above 1,000 feet.

Suggested Reading

Here are some other titles from Garden Way Publishing and Storey Publishing that can help you grow, prepare, and store your fresh produce. These books are available wherever quality books are sold. You may order directly by writing Storey Communications, Inc., P.O. Box 445, Pownal, Vermont 05261 or calling 800-441-5700.

Broccoli and Company, by Audra and Jack Hendrickson (#558-8)

Cold Climate Gardening, by Lewis Hill (#441-7)

Corn: Meals and More, by Olwen Woodier (#456-5)

Country Fresh Gifts, by the Editors of Garden Way Publishing (#660-6)

Down-to-Earth Gardening Know-How for the '90s, by Dick Raymond (#649-5)

The Elegant Onion, by Betty Cavage (#460-3)

The Harvest Gardener, by Susan McClure (#797-1)

Herbal Vinegar, by Maggie Oster (#843-9)

Joy of Gardening Cookbook, by Janet Ballantyne (#355-0)

Keeping the Harvest, by Nancy Chioffi and Gretchen Mead (#650-9)

Making and Using Dried Foods, by Phyllis Hobson (#615-0)

The New Zucchini Cookbook, by Nancy C. Ralston and Marynor Jordan (#589-8)

Peppers Hot and Sweet, by Beth Dooley (#621-5)

Root Cellaring, by Mike and Nancy Bubel (#703-3)

Simply Strawberries, by Sara Pitzer (#382-8)

Tomatoes, by the Editors of Garden Way Publishing (#672-X)

Mail-Order Sources of Preserving Equipment and Supplies

A Cook's Wares
211 37th St.
Beaver Falls, PA 15010-2103
412-846-9490
Appliances, gadgets

Gardener's Supply Company
128 Intervale Rd.
Burlington, VT 05401
800-444-6417
*Dehydrators, strainers, boilable
bags, and sealers*

Kitchen Krafts
P.O. Box 805
Mt. Laurel, NJ 08054
800-776-0575
Canning supplies, gadgets

Lemra Products
P.O. Box 186
Danielson, CT 06231
203-774-7024
*Manufacturer of Squeezo
Strainers*

Vermont Country Store
P.O. Box 300
Manchester Center, VT 05255-3000
802-362-2400
Miscellaneous equipment

Index

Page references in *italics* indicate illustrations;
page references in **bold** indicate tables.